God Bless you Louise

Come Climb The Ladder And Rejoice

The Prayer Life

Volume Two

By

Louise D'Angelo

Published By
THE MARYHEART CRUSADERS, INC.
22 Button Street
Meriden, Conn. 06450

Printed in U.S.A.

NIHIL OBSTAT: The Reverend Norman Belval, S.T.D.
                      Censor Deputatis

IMPRIMATUR: The Most Reverend John F. Whealon
                      Archbishop of Hartford, Conn.
                      April 15, 1990

The Nihil Obstat and Imprimatur are official declaration that a book or pamphlet is free of doctrinal or moral error.

Library of Congress No. 88-92302

ISBN 1-878886-02-9

Printed and bound in the United States of America.

TABLE OF CONTENTS

Preface   vii

Introduction   ix

PART ONE

Mental Prayer
Meditation
Contemplation

CHAPTER   PAGE

1. The Need For Mental Prayer   3

2. How To Practice Mental Prayer   9

3. The Rewards of Mental Prayer   17

4. Meditation   21

5. The Conversation: Christ Talks To The Soul   29

6. Contemplation   33

7. Those Who Are Ready For Contemplation   41

PART TWO

The Prayer Life Of Holy Abandonment

1. The Perfection Of Holy Abandonment.   51

2. Heroic Acts of Virtue   63

3. How To Prepare For The Prayer
   Of Holy Abandonment   75

4. The Busy Person And Interior Mortification   89
5. The Wondrous Fruits Of Holy Abandonment.   99

PART THREE

The Living Desert

Introduction.   149
1. The Living Desert   151
2. Preparation For The Living Desert State   155
3. Developing Signs   159
4. The Turning Point.   163
5. Pure Faith And Confidence   167
6. The Entrance Into The Living Desert   171
7. The Silence And Emptiness Of The Living Desert. . . .   175
8. More Insights Into The Living Desert   177
9. The Desert's Accessibility.   181
10. Walking Deeper Into The Living Desert   185
11. The Living Desert Expands.   189
12. The Living Desert Blooms   193
13. The Living Desert And Daily Life.   197
14. The Living Desert And Faults And Weaknesses.   201
15. Dealing With Remaining Faults And Weaknesses   205
16. The Living Desert And Crosses.   209
17. The Never-Ending Delights Of The Living Desert. . . .   213
18. The Final Stage Of The Living Desert:
    A Living Prayer.   217

PART FOUR
Heaven, Our Goal

1. Heaven, Our Goal 223
2. A Closer Look At Heaven 229
3. The Different Degrees Of Glory In Heaven 235
4. Grace And Eternal Happiness 243
5. Your Love For God In Heaven 249

Bibliography 253

Dedicated To All
Who Seek A Closer
Union With God

My Sincere Thanks
To Everyone Whose
Encouragement Made
This Book Possible

L. D.

ABOUT THE AUTHOR

Louise D'Angelo

Louise D'Angelo is the founder and president of an approved Catholic lay apostolate called "The Maryheart Crusaders." This non-profit organization has been in existence since 1964, and has received the acknowledgment of many Bishops in the United States. The main goal of The Maryheart Crusaders is to bring back fallen-away Catholics through a program of adult religious education; in addition, the organization strives to help improve the spiritual lives of Catholic lay people. The Crusaders' program includes meetings, lectures, classes for adults and distribution of free Catholic literature. Crusaders also defend the Pope, Bishops, priests, religious and deacons in various ways, for example, by letters to editors or to T.V. stations if and when these might attack the Catholic Church or its moral stands.

They participated in the Forty-first International Eucharistic Congress held in Philadelphia in 1976, at the Evangelization Conference in Washington D.C. in 1980, at several Marian congresses in the Boston area, and one in Hartford, Connecticut. Mrs. Louise D'Angelo is a nationally known writer and lecturer who has spoken at church affairs for many years. Her articles have appeared in such publications as *Marian Helpers Bulletin, Our Sunday Visitor, Immaculata* magazine, *The Mary-Heart Crusaders* newspaper, and *House of Loretto* magazine.

In addition, Mrs. D'Angelo is the author of the following books: *Too Busy for God? Think Again, Come Home. . .The Door Is Open* and *Mary's Light of Grace,* all published by The Maryheart Crusaders.

In keeping with her work as a Crusader, Louise has written against many cults, often doing extensive research. She is well qualified to bring to light the teachings of the Witnesses and to expose such teachings for all to see.

Her book, *The Catholic Answer to the Jehovah's Witnesses,* is her greatest effort concerning cults, and is presented to the public at a time when it is very much needed in order to challenge the Witnesses and their so-called "Bible truths."

PREFACE

Volume II

This book is a continuation of COME CLIMB THE LADDER AND REJOICE, Volume I. In the first volume, I explained how a person can start to climb THE LADDER OF PERFECTION to a closer union with God.

This book explains the different types and stages of a more advanced prayer life; and why it is so necessary to have an active prayer life as one struggles to, daily, climb that LADDER OF PERFECTION.

This book also explains the joys and peace found in the advanced forms of prayer and how to enter into such advanced forms of prayer.

From the first stages of prayer, called vocal prayers, to the highest forms of prayer called infused contemplation and Holy Abandonment, this book leads a person into areas which the person, perhaps, never realized existed, as he or she attempts to live a more active spiritual life.

In addition, the reader is introduced to an even higher prayer stage, which I call "The Living Desert." This form or stage of prayer becomes the golden chain binding all the forms of prayer into a union with God that is truly a dream-come-true for anyone, lay or religious, who seeks to find the perfection of personal union with God.

NEED FOR COMPETENT SPIRITUAL DIRECTOR

A word of caution: While the Holy Spirit plays an active roll in anyone's climb up THE LADDER OF PERFECTION, giving to the person many spiritual insights and understandings, it is most important to have a competent spiritual director who can examine such insights; especially in the areas of an advanced prayer life. Many insights which the person may receive as he or she takes this journey can easily be misunderstood and could lead the person astray. So tell your spiritual director what you goals are and let him guide you.

INTRODUCTION TO A MORE ACTIVE PRAYER LIFE

MARY'S ROLE

As I said, this book is a continuation of my book, COME CLIMB THE LADDER AND REJOICE, Volume I. The first book explained how a person can reach a closer union with God. This book brings the reader into the different stages of an active prayer life. But one cannot expect to go into the higher stages of prayer without Mary, the Mother of God.

For good reason, our Catholic Church encourages devotion to and love for Mary. She not only is there, as our own dear mother, to answer our prayers or to help us when we turn to her for strength to carry daily crosses, she also is ever ready to help us reach a closer union with God and to lead us into the higher stages of the prayer life.

No matter what stage of the prayer life one has entered, Mary is there. Mary becomes visible within a prayer life, as soon as the person says the Rosary for the very first time. That happens during the first stage called vocal prayer and continues right into the advanced stages of prayer. Never is the Rosary out of place in any prayer stage—not even the highest forms of contemplation.

If one is to follow Christ through each prayer stage, as THE LADDER OF PERFECTION is climbed, then one also needs Mary's hand to hold. For it is Mary who has left her examples to follow as the way and the means to be in tune with Christ. No one else can show the way to Christ as well as Mary whose dainty footsteps are to be found behind the footsteps of Christ.

There are many people, Protestants especially, who say that Mary is not needed in order to find Christ or to be united with Christ. They cast Mary aside and say: "I go straight to Christ." But all those people are wrong and they make a very serious mistake. They see Mary as an obstacle to a person's union with God; when in reality, Mary becomes the brilliant beacon of light revealing the pathway to that union. Why do I say that? Because God chose Mary to bring Christ to us.

The whole life of Christ from the moment of His conception to His death upon the cross was lived with Mary, His Mother, ever there, ever present within that life. And if we are to find our union with Christ, we also must make, within our spiritual lives, room for that ever-present Mother of the God whom we seek union with.

Something is lacking as they struggle along a road they are totally unfamiliar with; whereas, we, who hold Mary's hand, are led upon the paths which she knows so well.

Oh, we will have our own spiritual struggles, battles and problems, however, with Mary by our side, we know that we will not get lost in a darkness which hides the object of our affection from view.

As one travels through each stage of the prayer life, vocal prayer, mental prayer, meditation, contemplation, even the prayer of Holy Abandonment, Mary must be there lovingly encouraging the weakest of travelers to continue: "Don't give up, I will help you reach your goal. Have faith and trust in me."

Mary is not only needed to light the path which leads to union with Christ, but Mary is also a channel of grace. The one who was "filled with grace" when she walked the roads of life, brings tremendous graces to the souls of her beloved children who are so in need of these graces as they climb each rung of THE LADDER OF PERFECTION. Without such graces, no one could reach a very close union with God.

As these graces increase, and are used by the person, Mary's love for the individual is felt more intensely deep within the soul. The prayers said by the person, then receive the fine, delicate touches of this artist who knows what it means to give to and to receive from God, her Son, a wondrous love that will last for all eternity.

PART ONE

MENTAL PRAYER
MEDITATION
CONTEMPLATION

Chapter 1

THE NEED FOR MENTAL PRAYER

From vocal prayers, the prayer life advances into the areas of mental prayer and then into a more advanced form called meditation. Most prayer lives do not enter into these two stages. The majority of people, who pray, spend their entire lives repeating vocal prayers and they never know the wondrous joys of true mental prayer. The main reason for this neglect is lack of knowledge. They never knew that there is a stage of prayer called mental prayer. Others may have known but did not learn how to practice it. Still others may have given it a try but gave up when the first obstacle threw its menacing shadow upon the safe security of long-said, favorite prayers to the saints, novenas, or the Rosary. While such prayers can be most meritorious, as I said in the chapter on vocal prayer and are always needed in a well-balanced prayer life, there can be no spiritual growth if the person does not enter into mental prayer and meditation. Why is that? Mainly because, vocal prayers, even the Liturgy, the prayers during Mass, can become words spoken without a true, pure, love-filled contact with Christ.

While a person can express great love for Christ through vocal prayers, seldom, if ever, can the soul *experience* that love with only vocal prayers being said day in and day out. While a person can feel "close" to Christ or feel His presence when praying vocal prayers, there will always be something lacking within the prayer life if mental prayer is not part of that prayer life. In other words, mental prayer makes the prayer life far richer than does vocal prayer alone. So, if a person wants a more fuller, a more richer prayer life, mental prayer and meditation must become a part of

3

that prayer life. Vocal prayer introduces the person to Christ or our Lady or the saints; however, mental prayer brings the experience of their love to the depths of the soul.

That is why most people who have spent years or even a lifetime praying only vocal prayers, seldom, if ever, feel "loved" by God (or even our Lady) in such a way as to find a true lasting peace and joy in that love.

I remember that, for years, I was puzzled by the fact that many people, who were good Catholics, who went faithfully to Mass, who said the Rosary every day, showed very great defects in their whole spiritual relationship with God. For example, most of them never bothered to correct their most glaring faults and sins. Some did not even recognize such faults and sins. They seldom, if ever, found anything good in their lives and constantly presented, to whomever would listen, a never-ending list of trifle complaints and gossip. Many of these Catholics never understood the true meaning of Christian charity and were often very nasty to others. Others imagined that they "never did anything wrong," so why bother to go to confession? Often when a heavy cross was placed upon their shoulders, their reaction would be: "Is that the way God treats me after all I have done for Him?"

In addition, there are the "good" Catholics who stop going to Mass and stop praying when a loved one dies; as well as the ones who go to Mass but "get nothing" out of it.

As I said, the reactions and ways of such "good" Catholics used to puzzle me. Now I know the reasons for that type of unspiritual behavior. The Catholics, whom I have just described, never really learned what it meant to have a true, deep, lasting, love-filled relationship with Christ. In spite of all the vocal prayers said by them, they seldom, if ever, saw their own spiritual needs. Why? Because vocal prayers are what is known as "exterior prayers." That means that they can become disassociated with a person's interior spiritual life; so much so, that the person cannot see himself or herself as being in need of any spiritual improvement or advancement.

That is why, people who refuse to go to Mass, who refuse to receive the sacraments, who refuse to see their own sins and weaknesses, who will not leave a life of sin and corruption will still say: "Sure, I pray, in my own way." They may indeed say some prayers "in their own way"; however, the vocal prayers said by them never have the power to light up their interior life in such a manner as to reveal its true condition.

In like manner, people who are very busy but who sincerely want to "get closer to God," will become dissatisfied with and even frustrated by the fact that they never seem to improve themselves or their relationship with God in spite of all the Masses they attend and hurried Rosaries they say.

What happens to them is the exact same thing which happens to the "good" Catholics who cannot see their spiritual shortcomings and defects and to the fallen-away Catholics who pray in their "own way." Their vocal prayers cannot lead them into the depths of their spiritual relationship with God, because vocal prayers are and remain an exterior form of talking to God. They are the "on the surface" type of prayer which can become so automatic that the person does not even realize to whom he is talking when he prays.

That is the main reason why people find it so difficult to keep their minds on God or the words they say when they pray their vocal prayers. Everyone knows how easy it is to become distracted during Mass or when the Rosary is said. The length of the Mass or the Rosary is not the reason why. The reason is that the Mass and the Rosary are exterior vocal prayers which cannot bring into clear focus the main reason why one prays in the first place. That reason being to get in touch with God or Our Lady through words spoken and to pay attention to what one is saying, then to profit spiritually by such an encounter with the Lord. Very seldom can a person have a deep, lasting, meaningful encounter with Christ or our Lady through vocal prayers alone.

That explains why there are so many Catholics who easily stop praying or stop going to Mass when they blame God for all the miseries of their daily lives.

Also, that is why many Catholics are often accused of being hypocrites. It is said of them that they go to Mass every Sunday and then start on Monday to commit the sins they usually commit from Monday to the following Sunday. If they do not have a meaningful encounter with Christ during Mass, it is not too difficult to recognize their lack of spirituality as they ignore Christ and His teachings during the week.

It is safe to say that such Catholics, fallen-away Catholics, lukewarm Catholics, etc. never entered into the union with God called mental prayer. Why? Because, if they had advanced into mental prayer and meditation, they would have been more able to see, understand and correct their many un-Catholic ways, deeds, words and actions. There is such a refreshing sweetness found in mental prayer that when a soul experiences that delight, even briefly, the person will want to destroy the barriers which prevent that sweetness from covering the soul. He or she soon learns that faults, sins, weaknesses and so forth destroy the soul's ability to discover and possess that sweetness. Then the person has to be taught, by grace and knowledge, how to attempt to rid oneself of anything which clashes with the desires to taste and enjoy the wondrous fruits of peace, love and joy found in mental prayer. Then the soul's spiritual growth takes a giant leap upward. This experience of the sweetness of mental prayer is one far different than, say, the joys one can feel by and through vocal prayers. While vocal prayers can bring to the soul very warm moments of feeling close to Christ or to Mary, there is nothing to compare to the feelings of joys and closeness to Christ or to Mary found in mental prayer.

I believe that is one reason why average Catholics never go into the areas of mental prayer and meditation. They simply have nothing to compare their personal religious feelings and experiences with. If, on a given occasion, their souls are uplifted by a vocal prayer or a special Mass or a special public devotion, they think that is the utmost or ultimate in their union with God. However, as one sadly soon discovers such feelings seldom if ever last very long. When gone, the person is back again in the drudgery of daily living totally uninspired.

If such people only knew that the wondrous joys of mental prayer could be theirs every day, how much brighter life would become for them. Without this new and different type of deeper spiritual awareness, they simply do not know what they are missing. As a result, their faults, sins and failings, along with their un-Catholic ways, do not interfere with their prayer life because they can still say a "million" vocal prayers, they can still go to Mass, receive the Eucharist and say the Rosary without any knowledge or awareness that something is missing in their union with God.

Most Catholics will go to Mass, say morning and evening prayers, say the Rosary, etc. never knowing that there is a great deal more to prayer than the few vocal prayers which are their habit to say.

That does not mean that such vocal prayers are useless or wasted. Far from it. These vocal prayers do gain for Catholics many merits and graces. But it is sad to think of the untold graces and merits they could have had but which became lost to them, because they did not advance their prayer lives into the areas of mental prayer and meditation. The fact is, Saint Teresa of Avila, the great spiritual writer, maintains that vocal prayer alone can become so exterior, in relationship to God, that it becomes no prayer at all mainly because by and through vocal prayers the person merely repeats what someone else wrote or said. Thus, there is lacking in vocal prayers the personal direct conversation with Christ that can come only when mental prayer is used. St. Teresa insists that the prayer life must include mental prayer and meditation as well as vocal prayers; for a "million" vocal prayers can never take the place of the personal contact with Christ which is found only in mental prayer.

If the reader of this chapter, who has never practiced mental prayer, begins to think that he or she has missed something very important and very precious in the prayer life, that is correct. Why? Because vocal prayers can and often do lead a person into praying only with the lips and *not the heart as well.* Vocal prayers can also stop a person from the crucial examination of one's inner self which is needed to see and correct faults, weaknesses and sins. That is not the case with mental prayer. Because mental prayer directs the thoughts inward towards the God who dwells in a person's soul. Faults, failings and weaknesses can be more clearly seen because they do act as a barrier which hides the light of God's love from the person. That is why, as I said, mental prayer brings a desire to rid oneself of these obstacles which prevent a more complete union with the God who dwells deep within the soul. A reading of Saint Teresa's "Interior Castle" reveals just how many obstacles the soul finds as it struggles to know and love the God who dwells within the soul. Mental prayer not only brings into view a clearer picture of Christ's presence in the soul, but it also shows the person what prevents the light of His love from illuminating a daily life.

It is mental prayer which separates the "men from the boys" or the "adult from the child" in the prayer life. In other words, additional spiritual growth begins to take place when the person begins to practice mental prayer.

Chapter 2

HOW TO PRACTICE MENTAL PRAYER

Now that a person knows how important to his or her spiritual growth mental prayer is, the first question to ask is: how does one practice mental prayer?

First of all, realize that what a person seeks in mental prayer is not so much a new way to pray, but a new love-filled encounter with Christ. It is an entirely new experience, but with the same Christ or Mary one has found in vocal prayers. In vocal prayers, the person may have "talked" to Christ or Mary but the person can only feel the closeness to Christ or Mary which comes by and through mental prayer.

Both vocal and mental prayers are "talking to God," however, there is a very great difference between merely "talking to God" in vocal prayer and encountering Him in mental prayer. One can "talk to God" in vocal prayer but never really encounter Him. In other words, the person may never really know or understand whom it is he talks to. That is not the case with mental prayer or with meditation.

Notice that I separate the two, mental prayer and meditation. Most spiritual writers do not. So, in a chapter about mental prayer, you will find the words switching from mental prayer to meditation, all of which is supposed to mean one and the same thing. I find a difference between the two in degree at least. Mental prayer is a lower form of meditation or just one part of meditation. Mental prayer requires more of a preparation and effort than does meditation. Also mental prayer is but the beginning of meditation.

With that difference in mind, I will explain about the way to start one's spiritual climb into the areas of mental prayer.

First of all, mental prayer is something apart or different than what one usually finds in a well-balanced spiritual program. It is an addition to such a program. It is not spiritual reading, an examination of conscience (necessary for a valid confession) or thinking about good intentions. It is not a so-called "born again" experience. It does not "just come" naturally. It must be taught to a person who then must practice it. There might be great difficulty adding this type of prayer to a spiritual program. On the other hand, many Catholics may have already engaged in a bit of mental prayer and had not even known it.

For example, if a person has, after receiving the Eucharist during Mass, returned to his seat, closed his eyes and adored the Lord who came to him, that person has experienced one type of mental prayer. If a person lingers in Church after Mass to talk to Christ in the tabernacle, again that is a form of mental prayer. If a person pauses while saying a vocal prayer to think deeply about what has just been said, that person also has touched the borders of mental prayer.

Notice now the differences between vocal prayers and the examples of mental prayer which I have just given. The main difference is the absence of prayers which someone else wrote which the person used in order to "talk to God."

Mental prayer then becomes a very personal, interior encounter with Christ with the person praying in his or her "own way" without the use or aid of Rosaries, prayer books, prayer cards or Sunday Missals. It is talking to God in the person's own words after the person has mentally placed himself or herself in the presence of God.

However, mental prayer is far more than "talking to God" in the person's own way. It is not just mentally placing oneself in the presence of God. It is to actually experience God's presence as the person talks to him. That is what separates the borderline mental prayers from true mental prayers.

I can explain the difference between vocal and mental prayers in another way by saying that when we pray with vocal prayers, we "bring" God to us as we try to capture His presence by the words we say. When we use mental prayer, we must first of all "go" to God before we start talking to Him. In other words, in vocal prayers we start to pray before we feel or know that God is near us. With mental prayer, we know that God is near us before we start to pray.

Some people think that vocal prayers are only prayers said out loud and mental prayers are the ones we say in our minds without moving our lips. However, if the prayer, said in the mind, is one written by someone else, taken from a prayer book or the Rosary, all such prayers remain vocal and not mental. Even when a mystery of the Rosary is thought about while saying the Our Father or Hail Mary, the thoughts become part of the vocal prayer.

True mental prayer is something that does not come instantly to a person; although as I said, some people may have touched the borders of mental prayer and not known it. A person must be introduced to mental prayer and taught how to use it. A person must practice mental prayer and it could take a long time before the person feels comfortable with this type of spiritual exercise. A person must find time for mental prayer often far more time than is spent with a quick vocal prayer or a fast Rosary. A person must prepare himself for a period of mental prayer. Such a preparation is different than one for vocal prayers when a person merely picks up the Rosary or a prayer book. And this preparation must begin with silence. Why? Because Christ dwells deep within the silence in the soul and it is there where one finds a loving encounter with the Lord. The main reason why most people never really get to know the Lord who dwells within their own souls is that these people never discover the silence wherein He dwells.

Our world is such a noisy one! It is filled with all sorts of activities. Most people, especially with families, find it almost impossible to find a moment of peace and quiet during the day. There are loud radio programs or T.V. programs to shatter silence. There are conversations, arguments, disagreements and so forth. In addition, most people are plagued with a wide variety of inner conflicts, fears, worries, torments and anxieties. All these produce exterior and also interior noises. Vocal prayers add to all that noise, which is why it is very necessary to practice mental prayer.

Even if vocal prayers are said in the mind, with no words spoken out loud, your inner self clearly hears the noise of your vocal prayers because your will, your intellect, your mind, your whole being are all active in one way or another and this activity produces noise. It is this noise which prevents a close, love-filled encounter with Christ who dwells deep within the silence of your own soul. One of the main purposes for practicing mental prayer is to discover the silence within your being where Christ dwells.

In order to better understand what I have just explained, try this little experiment. Take a Rosary in your hand and say ten Hail Marys. Notice that the vocal prayers, the Hail Marys call to attention your will, your intellect, your mind, your heart, etc. Even deep within your being, the noise or activity of your vocal prayers is there. Your whole being has been called to attention to listen to the vocal prayers. One reason why there are so many distractions during vocal prayers, the Mass or the Rosary is that there are "a million" other thoughts in your mind which also are calling for your attention. It is very easy to jump from one thought to another because that only becomes part of the activity produced by the vocal prayer. It is like ten people talking to you at once. They all want your attention, but you do not know whom to listen to first. So your attention switches from one to another. While there may still be distractions during mental prayer, especially when you are a beginner, these spiritual disturbances will be far less as you attempt to pay attention to only one subject: the Christ who dwells within your soul.

To continue with the little experiment, go into a silent room (no noise whatsoever) sit or kneel in a comfortable position and close your eyes. Take your beloved Rosary and just hold it in your hands. Do not say any of its prayers but feel the comfort it brings to you. Now clear your mind of all thoughts. This is called interior mortification. Then pick out your favorite mystery of the Rosary. Say that is the Nativity. Start to think about the Nativity and nothing else. Let all worries, daily events, conversations, etc.

fade from your mind. Allow your mind to pay attention to only one thing: the Nativity. Do not pray, just think about the wondrous birth of Christ. See Mary and Joseph kneeling next to the Child in the Manger. Then, in your mind, join them. Place yourself next to the manger and just love the Christ Child, with your whole heart: *without saying a word!*

Suddenly you will notice one very striking element of mental prayer. You will be enveloped in silence. This silence will be so profound that it could very well frighten you. It will be something you never experienced before. It will be so new and different that you might want to jump up to rush back into your familiar world of exterior and interior noises.

But, on the other hand, you might just taste a bit of the wondrous sweetness and closeness to Christ which are impossible to taste in vocal prayer.

Before I continue, let me again point out that, while speaking of mental prayer, I am not downgrading vocal prayer. Vocal prayer is very important in a complete prayer life. Surely we need the Mass, the Rosary and many other written types of prayers from ones of adoration to ones of thanksgiving. Mental prayer is an addition to the prayer life. The fact is, unless a person is well-advanced in the vocal-prayer stage of spiritual development, that person could never handle or understand mental prayer. So do not give up vocal prayer in favor of mental prayer. Both are necessary in a well-balanced prayer life.

Once you have discovered the silence necessary for mental prayer, you can begin to formulate a method of mental prayer.

THE METHOD

The method, and there are several which were written by different saints, helps you to reach your goal of mental prayer which is to have a love-filled encounter with the Christ who dwells in your soul. One such method was developed by Saint Ignatius Loyola, another by Saint Teresa of Avila and still another by Saint Francis de Sales.

All three methods produce the same result and are basically the same; so I will just give a summary of them.

1. The first step is to find a place where you can be alone and pray in silence. The best place would be a Church when everyone else has left. But you may not always be able to go to Church just for mental prayer. A little-used room in your home would be a suitable place. Also, the time you choose for mental prayer is just as important as the place. One priest who wrote a book on mental prayer said that the best time for him to pray was in the morning. He said that in the evening he was simply too tired to keep his mind on the subject he chose for mental prayer. Lay people might find that the best time for them, for this type of prayer, is in the evening, after the family has gone to bed and all is quiet and peaceful. Just remember that whatever time and place suits you best, you must place yourself in an environment of silence.

2. The second step is to still your thoughts until you clear your mind of all distractions. It will help you to do that if you remember that you are preparing yourself to talk to Christ and all other thoughts will compete for your attention and take your mind away from Christ. Clearing your mind of all distractions may be very difficult at first and you will no doubt discover that you can still your mind for only a minute or two at first. Then wild thoughts will rush in to demand your attention. The fact is, you will no doubt use up the time allotted for your mental prayer just trying to get rid of all the distractions in your mind. But do not give up. Practice does make perfect, and the longer you practice this interior mortification, the easier it will become.

3. The next step is to select the subject matter for your mental prayer. There are numerous events in the life of Christ which can become the subject for your mental prayer. For example, you can think about the birth of Christ or His death. The Mysteries of the Rosary are an excellent source of events in the life of Christ, so is the Bible. Once you have chosen the subject matter, then you can take the next step.

4. With the picture clearly in your mind, close your eyes and imagine that you are there with Christ or Mary. This part of the method for mental prayer is called the "imagination." With your imagination you can form all sorts of activities connected with

the subject you have chosen. For example, you can become part of the crowd which actually witnessed a great miracle of Christ's. You can share the people's awe, excitement and joy.

5. Next comes the part of the method called "consideration." Think about the event pictured in your mind and try to find the meaning. But do not look for the meaning in relationship to the world or what the event meant to the people who were there when it happened. Look for a very personal meaning. Ask yourself, what does this event mean to me? If you are thinking of the crucifixion, ask yourself: "Can it be that Christ went through all that suffering just for me?" The answer is yes, He did. If you are thinking of the resurrection, then say to yourself: "Christ rose from the dead to prove He was God. What joy to know that I am so loved by Christ that He, my God, came to save me."

6. Up to this point, you have not really prayed to Christ. You have not gone into mental prayer. You have only prepared yourself for your prayer or conversation with Christ. Now comes the prayer. With the subject matter very clear in your mind, you can now talk to Christ in your "own way." You do not need a prayer book or even a Rosary. You have placed yourself in the presence of Christ who will now cease His activities to listen to what you want to say to Him.

7. What do you say to Him? Talk about the mental picture you have formed in your imagination. If the picture was of His birth, tell Him of the joy you feel because He so loved you that He willed to be born, to come to earth, to save you. Keep your prayer around the event you have chosen to place in your mind. At the beginning, you may not know what to say. You may not be able to express your feelings in words. But that does not matter. Just love Christ. In your mind, just look at Him with love. The look becomes a prayer in itself.

8. Then the final step is what is called the "conclusion." Go over in your mind your whole preparation and conversation with Christ. Think about the fact that you, a mere creature of the Creator, had the wondrous privilege of actually talking to God.

Now, these eight steps of the method for mental prayer may, at first, seem rather lengthy and complicated but that is only when you are a beginner. The longer you practice this type of prayer, the better able you will be to quickly gather your thoughts together for your chosen period of mental prayer. Also, you can arrange your own method with your spiritual director. What I just gave you was an idea or example of the correct method for mental prayer.

Chapter 3

THE REWARDS OF MENTAL PRAYER

As I said, in the previous chapter, when a person uses vocal prayers, he or she attempts to capture Christ's presence by the words he says. On the other hand, when the person gets involved in mental prayer, he or she has to "find" Christ before a conversation, a prayer, can be said.

It is very important, in mental prayer, to "find" Christ before you talk to Him. That is why you use a method which prepares you for the mental prayer. The method allows you to search for and find Christ who already dwells in your soul through sanctifying grace. This search for Christ is but one of the many rewards of mental prayer. It makes you stop and think deeply about Christ before you attempt to talk to Him. Such a search does not come when you say only vocal prayers. How many people actually prepare themselves for an encounter with Christ during Mass? Not very many. Most rush to Church for Mass, start talking to someone before Mass begins, and rush out of Church after Mass. How many people search for Christ before they start vocal prayers? Again, not very many. So the search for Christ, by means of the preparation or the method for mental prayer becomes a very inspiring reward of that type of prayer. It, so to say, puts you in the correct mood for prayer.

Another, very important, reward for mental prayer is the fact that the preparation becomes a practice of two very important virtues. These are interior mortification and detachment from the distractions of daily living. If practiced long enough to acquire these two spiritual skills, you can use them often, even during the whole day to live a more spiritual life.

The interior mortification is often called recollection by spiritual writers. It is the virtue of interior mortification which drives out of your mind useless thoughts, unnecessary worries and anxieties. If you form a habit of casting aside these useless thoughts *as soon as* they begin to take control of your mind, you will be better able to say little prayers called ejaculations. Once these brief prayers, said as you carry out the duties of your daily life, become part of your routine, you will find the actual preparation for mental prayer much easier to make.

These two virtues, interior mortification and detachment, can also be used to improve the quality of your vocal prayers. Vocal prayers which had been said poorly can become more meaningful and gain far more merits once the mind is free from distractions.

Another wondrous reward for saying or engaging in mental prayer is an increase of love for God. It is a well-known fact among spiritual writers that the less one thinks of Christ or Mary, the less the person will love them. You cannot have much love in your heart for Christ or Mary if you don't really know them well. How much love can a person have for Christ who suddenly becomes present to the person during a Mass and then quickly disappears from view with the last amen? Not very much. How do you get to know Christ and Mary better? It is through prayer.

But not just a once-a-week prayer. Prayer is not only talking to Christ or Mary but it is thinking about them as well, it is learning more about them through spiritual reading. It is bringing them into your daily lives to share that life with you. Now, I am not talking about being fanatical. Remember, there is always a correct way and a wrong way to grow more spiritually. The wrong way is to become so fanatical about religion that everything in your life is excluded. Christ wants us all to live our daily lives faithfully carrying out all our duties and obligations. To think about Christ or Mary or a beloved saint during the day and sharing your life with them is not being fanatical. That becomes a sincere desire to know them better so you can love them more.

There are many other rewards to find if you do not become discouraged and give up mental prayer when difficulties arise. Saint Peter of Alcantara tells us that by and through mental prayer all virtues are purified and polished. Slowly but surely, a person's faith increases as his desire to speak to Christ increases. His hope becomes brighter as he realizes that his love for Christ is not one-sided. He discovers that Christ returns love for love. He begins to discover that many things he had thought to be so important in life, such as petty arguments and disagreements which can throw a person into a state of depression, are not really that important after all.

As the person's desire for the silence of mental prayer increases, he will discover how much time he wastes during each day by useless conversations or watching T.V. programs which cannot inspire him to live a holier life.

There is a story told about Saint Teresa and her father. He would often visit his daughter in her convent and speak about unimportant, daily interests and events. Then she introduced him to mental prayer and taught him the correct methods of mental prayer. She soon discovered that his visits to her became less and less. He began to find such joy and delights in mental prayer that he considered talking about trivial matters a waste of time.

Also, a person who practices mental prayer daily will want to examine his whole way of life in order to regulate it more, put it in order, separate what is important from what is useless and a waste of time.

Once the person tastes the sweetness and delights found in having a personal conversation with Christ or Mary or a beloved saint, that person will be able to face daily crosses and problems with a new, beautiful attitude of acceptance. He might even discover that a cross which he thought to have been so heavy to carry now becomes lighter for he knows that Christ is present to help him with his burden.

In addition, once a person finds Christ in mental prayer, he begins to want to learn more about Christ and his beautiful Catholic religion. There arises a hunger which leads to more and better spiritual reading. A person then starts to realize how poor were his reading habits. He might have read only the daily newspaper or a sports magazine or even a magazine filled with suggestive pictures which bring very un-Christ-like thoughts to him.

But suddenly that type of reading leaves him empty and his deep spiritual needs unfulfilled. So he will begin to seek out books about our faith or stories about our saints. He will surely want to learn more about the wonders and joys of mental prayer.

As his soul advances up THE LADDER OF PERFECTION through mental prayer, the person will want to find other ways to bring himself into a closer union with God. So he starts to see his own faults and failings in a different light, one which reveals their true nature. Then he begins to develop a keener sense of what might be lacking in his spiritual life.

However, the most important and wondrous rewards of mental prayer comes from a true spiritual awakening. The person will actually experience the joys and begin to taste the sweetness of a personal encounter with Christ who dwells within the soul.

This, of necessity, must come very slowly and gradually. Christ does not just "burst" upon a soul to reveal the spiritual sweetness of His presence. Christ will reveal Himself to a soul only to the degree that the person has been prepared to accept and understand such an encounter.

The so-called, "born again," sudden spiritual awakenings which some people experience are but a beginning of an encounter with Christ. Unfortunately, most people who have such an experience tend to regard it as the beginning and end, all wrapped up in one spiritual package. That is not true for there is much work to be done to actually bring the soul into a very close union with Christ. Christ does not blind His children with the brightness of His presence. He allows only a tiny bit of His light to show at one time. The person will see the rays become brighter and brighter only after much preparation and prayer. That is why many people who do have a "born again" experience begin after a period of time to lose the excitement and joy of that moment. So they attempt to preserve or recapture that moment, usually making many spiritual mistakes simply because of lack of knowledge as to the next step to take up THE LADDER OF PERFECTION. One of the first and most important steps to take is the daily practice of mental prayer.

Chapter 4

MEDITATION

The next step to take to improve or add to your prayer life is what is known as meditation. As I said, I separate mental prayer and meditation, although meditation is part of mental prayer. Before I go into the subject of meditation, I wish to give a quick review of the method for mental prayer. This will give you a way to more clearly see the difference between mental prayer and meditation.

Mental prayer requires a period of preparation such as going into a silent room or Church, fixing in your mind a mental picture of Christ, thinking deeply about this mystery, and talking to Christ about the event in His life.

Meditation also requires a period of preparation but this preparation need not be as extensive or as formal as the one for a beginner's period of mental prayer. By the time a person is ready for the prayer stage of meditation, he will be able to quickly place himself in the proper state of recollection needed for meditation. This ability is the direct result of the practice of mental prayer. And unless a person has practiced mental prayer for a period of time, he cannot go into meditation. Make no mistake about that. Do not try to place yourself in a prayer state of meditation unless you have a great deal of experience in the lower forms of mental prayer.

Although some people say they meditate during or after vocal prayer, this type of a meditation is not what they say it is. There is a very definite difference between true meditation and what the person may want to believe is meditation. This same type of mistake or confusion is also found with the highest form of mental prayer called contemplation. Many people think they are ready for contemplation when they do not even know what mental prayer is. One day a religious, who was teaching a prayer class of adults said to me: "Well, my class is ready for contemplation. They want to know how to contemplate." Knowing him and his class of lay people, I asked: "How can they go into the areas of contemplation when you have never taught them the correct methods for mental prayer?" He answered: "Oh, the Holy Spirit will lead them into contemplation."

Although I did respect his enthusiasm and sincerity, I rather doubted that the Holy Spirit would rush a soul into true contemplation when the soul was never prepared for such a lofty height of spiritual union with God.

A person may feel a tremendous surge of joy when he or she suddenly discovers that there is a Christ who actually does love him or her; however, such a feeling is never lasting unless the person begins to build a genuine, correct prayer life upon that foundation. The true state of contemplation is so exalted that a person would not even want to desire that state when far from prepared to enter into it. Also, it is something a person cannot bring himself or herself into as I will explain in the chapter on contemplation.

No stage of the prayer life can be pushed aside or skipped; because, from the simplest vocal prayer to the height of prayer called Holy Abandonment, there are many valuable lessons to be learned in each stage. Until such lessons are learned, the person is not ready for the next step up the ladder of prayer.

This same rule applies to all areas of living, growing, going to school, going to college and learning a job in a factory or office. A child cannot go to college until he has passed through the lower grades of school. Likewise, a man or woman cannot enter into the higher forms of mental prayer until he or she is quite familiar with the lower forms. If the person attempts to jump from vocal prayers into the areas of contemplation, that person would not be able to understand what is in the world of contemplation, in much the same way, that a child of ten could never understand what is taught in a college classroom.

For example, in mental prayer the person discovers that Christ dwells within his or her own soul. In meditation, the person learns how to love the Christ who is discovered in the soul. How could the person fall in love with Christ if he or she never even knew He existed?

Now you can better understand why the mental pictures of Christ found in the lower forms of mental prayer are so very important inasmuch as they make the person more aware of who Christ really is and what He did. Only then can the man or woman begin to learn to love Christ.

That "falling in love with Christ" is where I place the separation between the lower forms of mental prayer and meditation. A person can enter into mental prayer and be very sincere about his or her desires to become closer to Christ and yet never really love Christ. A person can talk to Christ by and through mental prayer but never really love Him. A person can deeply respect Christ, while mental prayers are said but still never experience a ray of love for Him. A person can speak words of love to Christ in mental prayer but never really mean what the words of love are supposed to mean. In other words, a person can think about Christ, form a mental picture of Him and pray to Him with lips and not with the heart as well.

When a person enters into meditation, then the heart begins to come alive as the soul responds to grace. In the lower forms of mental prayer, the beginner discovers that he or she spends a great deal of the prayer period *thinking* about Christ and forming a mental picture of Him. Now, in the areas of meditation, the person spends less time *thinking* about Christ and more time loving Him.

No one need tell the person that love for Christ is developing and expanding in his heart. No one need tell the person that he or she is becoming more and more aware of Christ's love for him or her. The person will know that himself. If the person must ask: "Do I really love Christ? Does Christ love me," that person has not experienced the type of love I am talking about. When that happens, the wondrous sweetness and joy of that love will be discovered. For that love is not a struggle to gain, it is not an empty type of love, it is not a one-sided love. It is not even an over-powering love which is experienced by the "born again" or charismatic type of Christian. I am always a little bit suspicious of that type of sudden love for Christ. While it can be a genuine religious experience, it can also do a great deal of damage to a person's spiritual life if not handled correctly. I know many Catholics who were once excellent Catholics but who lost their Catholic faith after they had had a "born again" experience. They felt that they "had" Christ and the Holy Spirit so they no longer needed the Church and the sacraments. Of course, they were sadly mistaken.

So that is not the type of love for Christ which comes from meditation. The love I am talking about is a very hidden, silent love which the person wants to hide from the eyes of the world. It is a very deep, personal love which is too precious, too beauti-ful to share with anyone except perhaps the person's spiritual director. It is the type of love which draws the person into more frequent periods of meditation. The person will want to withdraw more and more from the noises of the world to be alone with his or her beloved Lord because there is so much sweetness and joy found in that encounter and aloneness.

Once this type of love-filled encounter with Christ captures the person's heart and soul, the prayer of meditation will carry the person into yet another area of spiritual growth. The person will begin to discover that there are many barriers to a fuller, more complete union with God. These obstacles will consist of all sorts of things which hinder the soul's progress up THE LADDER OF PERFECTION.

The person may find his love for Christ, or the love he wants to give to Christ, mixed with a "million" other loves which now become "out of tune" with the sweet melody of a pure, holy love for Christ. There may be in a person's life a variety of strong loves and affections which are opposed to Christ's ways and teachings. For example: a person may have too great an affection for or attachment to such things as beautiful clothes, fine foods, sports, furniture, all sorts of items which a person has or desires to possess. A person may have a strong love for daily T.V. programs which he or she will spend hours watching. A person may have a great love for gossip and spend hours on the phone or with a neighbor talking about others. A person may be filled with love for a certain knowledge which he or she may possess and in that way always wants to appear superior to others. A person might have a love for his own ideas and opinions and refuse to listen to advice or to admit that he may be wrong. All such loves and affections are cemented to a person's heart and act as a hindrance to loving Christ as He should be loved. Meditation helps to slowly but surely chisel away that hard crust which surrounds the heart. As each love or affection is discovered, the person can pray for the graces to remove it from his life so that he can give a more complete, less divided, purer love to Christ.

When that happens, when the rays of love from the person's heart are less divided, the person will discover another marvelous reward or fruit of meditation. The person will find a greater, purer love in his heart not only for Christ and Mary but for his dear loved ones as well. He will begin to realize how precious are the close members of his family and his dear friends. He will begin to see the love which he had for them but which was hidden. He will look beyond the daily crosses and problems of his daily life and discover a loved one whom he never really saw before; even though, the person was there right next to him all the time.

Often men and women will spend a lifetime chasing dreams which are supposed to bring "eternal" happiness. Yet, at the same time, they overlook and neglect the very ones in their daily lives, the members of their own families, who are more than willing to shower upon them the love and care needed for that happiness.

Most people have a very serious fault of constantly looking for their happiness in a dream world which does not and never will exist. There are the ones who dream of winning a million dollars and then spend years wasting precious time thinking about what they would do with all that money. People who live in a dream world waiting each moment for their lives to change into a "paradise," make a very serious mistake. They can see nothing good in their daily lives or no one who really cares about them. Some people spend their whole lives never once saying thank you to

God for the good things in their lives. They are too busy looking for and even praying for their own personal "Garden of Eden."

The proper use of meditation can cure that type of spiritual illness. The person will discover that all loves, dreams and affections which compete for and with the love Christ wants from the person will have to disappear. This eradication and uprooting may be very painful at first, but as the person's prayer life progresses, the person will not only get rid of such spiritual illnesses, but will end up wondering why on earth he or she allowed such barriers to enter in the first place.

For example: I know a person who had a habit of watching the late news on T.V. every evening. The news started at 10:00 p.m. After that news broadcast ended, she felt she had to switch to another station to watch the 11:00 p.m. news. When that ended at 11:30 p.m., she felt she had to go to another station to pick up the 11:30 p.m. news there. She felt she did not want to miss any news; yet she did not realize she was hearing the same news over and over. This went on for about one year until the woman suddenly decided to turn the T.V. off at 11:00 p.m. and say a few prayers. Then she quickly went through a few vocal prayers so she could look at the 11:30 p.m. news.

Gradually she stopped the 11:30 p.m. news and continued to pray. Grace began to work as she responded to the wondrous graces found in prayer. She discovered that seeing all the news broadcasts was not really that important after all. She planned for herself a very meaningful prayer program using the time she once spent looking at all the news on T.V. One year later she could not understand why she had wasted such precious time looking at all the news when she could have been praying.

Another man I know was caught up in the wild and un-Catholic ways of a tough truck driver. He loved to be with "the boys" talking about very un-Christian subjects, doing his share of cursing. Then one day, he responded to grace and began a meaningful prayer life which included mental prayer and meditation. After he had found his joy and peace with the Lord, he made a startling discovery. He had kept his truck driving job but had spent less and less time talking "to the boys." Then one day, he was in the same room with them listening to their wild talk, curses and jokes. Suddenly, a great fear gripped his heart as he said to himself: "My dear Lord! Was I really like that? Is that the way I used to talk and act?" He could hardly believe that indeed he had been "one of the boys." He made up his mind never, never to become like that again.

That is one of the wondrous rewards of meditation. Unlike vocal prayers which people can stop at any given moment for any poor excuse, the prayer of meditation brings lasting love for Christ and a *lasting change* in daily habits from bad to good or from good to better.

There are more rewards of meditation which the person finds delight in discovering. As the person understands who Christ really is and what He did, as the person learns about pure love for Christ and from Him, the person will realize a very important fact. The Christ whom is now more fully understood and loved is also the Christ who is an example to follow! Christ's ways, then, become a goal to reach. If a person is to truly love Christ, then that person must also follow His ways and teachings.

When the person has reached this stage of spiritual development, he will then be able to take a good, honest look at himself and see more clearly his own sins, faults and weaknesses. He will also have desires to become more Christ-like and to live a more Christ-centered life.

The reason for that is obvious. Faults, sins, failings and weaknesses all become sour notes in the melody of love sung between the soul and Christ.

If, for example, the person while meditating, pours out his or her love for Christ and at the same time never bothers to see and correct faults and sins, then there is good reason for Christ to doubt the sincerity of that love. Or, if a person knows he is attached to certain sins and refuses to give them up by acquiring and practicing virtues, what kind of a love could that person offer to Christ? Such a half-love, insincere love cannot enter into the areas of meditation. Why? Because then the sweetness and joys found in meditation simply would not be there. Such sweetness and joys can only come from the purity of the soul's love for

Christ and Christ's love for the soul. Within that purity is to be found sincerity and honesty. There can be no pretense or deceit in such a spiritual relationship. And if the person honestly wants the type of relationship with Christ found in meditation, that person must become aware of his or her sins, faults and failings and seek ways and means to correct the same as soon as possible.

True love is always proven by tenderness, care and attention to the one who is loved. It is also shown by pleasing the beloved one. If one is to please Christ, the person, of necessity, must give up all which would displease Him.

The first virtue which a person must acquire and polish has to be charity. Charity, love for others, is but a pure expression of love for Christ. A person cannot love Christ and at the same time hate another person. Christ told us to make our peace with others before we bring our offering to Him at the altar. A person must enter into the love-encounter with Christ in meditation with a heart and mind completely free from all stains of bitterness, hate, jealousy or envy. These become the sour notes of a beautiful love song between the soul and Christ, and are very easily recognized.

A person cannot expect to conquer all his sins, faults and failings at once. That is not possible. But as the love for Christ, in the person's heart, becomes purer, as the person goes deeper into meditation, the person will find the graces needed to become more Christ-like and to live a more Christ-centered way of life. In other words, the advanced stages of prayer, such as deep meditation bring into the person's daily life a complete change for the better. Meditation brings to the person the desires to live a Christ-centered life. That being the case, the prayer of meditation becomes a way of life. It is not just something which happens at a certain time on a certain day. It is deep within your heart and soul as you carry out the daily duties and responsibilities of your daily life.

Chapter 5

THE CONVERSATION:
CHRIST TALKS TO THE SOUL

After a person becomes familiar with the preparations for mental prayer and meditation, the person will learn not only how to *talk to Christ* but how to *listen* to Him as well.

First, a word of warning! Please, *do not* expect to actually hear Christ speak to you with words that you will hear with your bodily ears. I am not talking about visions or divine messages such as were imparted to the saints. There are numerous people who have very vivid imaginations or mental or emotional problems who "tell the world" about their so-called "visions" and "messages" from "the Lord." Some of these false visionaries even attract a large following consisting of loyal devotees who promote all sorts of false "messages." Even when the Church condemns the visionary and the messages, disobedient followers insist that the Church is wrong and the one who claims visions is correct. A person must always, and I repeat, *always,* stay away from visions and "messages" from the Lord in his or her own personal spiritual life. Such extraordinary paths are not for the average person. Very, very few people are chosen to give to the world heavenly messages. And even for them, that path of spirituality becomes beset with numerous dangers. Also, no matter how many visions saints see, they must still come down to our level of following the ordinary means of sanctification. They still must find their graces and holiness by and through living an active prayer life, which includes the sacraments.

Contrary to popular beliefs, visions and heavenly messages do not constitute true sanctity. A saint is never canonized just because he or she saw visions. A saint becomes a saint by faithfully fulfilling and carrying out his or her daily religious and other duties and obligations.

That fact brings us down to our own paths to union with God, which includes a very active, true, pure prayer life.

As I said, after a person familiarizes himself with the preparations for mental prayer and meditation, the person will learn how to listen to Christ, as well as to talk to Him. What that means, to listen to Christ, is that the person will receive a great deal of self-knowledge so as to discover faults, weaknesses, etc., and know what graces to pray for. In addition, the person will become filled with wondrous insights so as to more fully understand Christ, what He did, why He did it, what He taught and how to live a more Christ-centered life.

When that begins to happen, the person's spiritual eyes will open so that he or she can begin to view life and living more through the eyes of God instead of through finite, limited, poor human reasoning.

Just remember that any conversation is a two-way affair. You may have a great many things to tell the Lord but remember that He also has a great many things to tell you, so learn how to *listen* to the Lord as well as talk to Him.

Begin the listening part of your mental prayers, by plunging your whole being into silence. You are never going to hear what Christ wants you to know if you do not, first of all, silence your own thoughts, desires and problems. Just sit and listen as you would to anyone who is telling you something you want to hear. Pay close attention to the insights and self-knowledge which the Lord is revealing to you. This type of "listening to the Lord" is far different from actual visions or messages and I will add: far less dangerous. It is making you realize what is wrong with or what is right about your spiritual life.

Also, when you allow the Lord to talk to you by and through your mental prayers, you will begin to discover many of His blessings in your daily life which you never paid any attention to before. You will begin to appreciate "little things" which you never thought were, in reality, God's gifts to you. You will learn that He, the great, the Almighty Lord of all, is actually interested in you as a person, as His own beloved child. He will show you signs of His love and affection for you, which suddenly make you realize that you are not alone in the vast vale of tears called life.

He will speak unspoken words, to you, of comfort, joy, consolation and pure love. You will "hear" such words by the reaction of your own heart responding to the warmth of His tenderness, goodness and grace. Remember that He wants to share His life with you and He is interested in you as a person.

Another way Christ "speaks" by and through mental prayers is when He speaks to us with His words in the Bible.

The Bible is the living word of God. If we spend part of our meditation thinking about some words which Christ spoke, which are recorded in the Bible, we can be sure that He is saying the same words to us. For example: Christ said: "I am the way, the truth and the life . . ." (*John* 14:6). When He speaks to us in mental prayer, saying such words, they are meant for us, for you and me. He is also speaking directly to us when He says such things as: "I give you a new commandment: love one another. Such as my love has been for you, so must your love be for each other . . . This is how all will know you for my disciples, your love for one another" (*John* 13:34-35).

There are numerous other words of Christ, in the Bible, which we can accept as His words to us when we "hear" them spoken by Christ during our mental prayers.

Finally, Christ also speaks to us by and through the Church. If the Church tells us that we must believe in Heaven, Hell and Purgatory, we can be sure that Christ is speaking to us telling us the same thing. If we "listen" to Christ talk to us while thinking of one or another of the Church's teachings, we can be sure that to obey such teachings is to obey Christ, to love such teachings is to love the things Christ tells us, and to follow such teachings is to follow Christ.

Chapter 6

CONTEMPLATION

The next step up the ladder of prayer which a person can enter into is called contemplation. I place this prayer stage after mental prayer and meditation, but before the highest form of prayer called Holy Abandonment.

Contemplation belongs more to the prayer-stage called Holy Abandonment than to the states of mental prayer and meditation. Yet, many spiritual writers merely include contemplation as part of mental prayer. While it can be called a part of mental prayer, it is as different from mental prayer and meditation as day is from night. It is in a class all by itself and chances are, the average lay person may never experience true infused contemplation. The reason being, that most contemplatives are religious who have a total contemplative life in a convent or monastery. Contemplation then is not only a prayer stage or state, but a way of life as well.

However, there have been and no doubt are today many contemplatives who are plain, ordinary lay people. So the life of contemplative prayer may be experienced if not by the majority of lay people, at least by a chosen few. And even if a person never experiences this state prayer, at least we can all understand what it is all about.

Now, when a person considers the word contemplation, he usually falls into two distinct categories. Number one, he imagines that the realm of contemplation is so far above him that he could not possibly reach such heights; or number two, he thinks he is already there. It seems to be that there are no in-betweens when contemplation is brought into the picture. Yet, there are, in reality, many in-betweens or different experiences of contemplation.

For example: if you ever went into a Church to pray and found no words to say, if you merely sat in the wondrous silence of the Divine Presence, if you felt a warm glow of His love capture your whole being and raise your soul to Heaven, you have experienced a tiny touch of contemplation. That is one of the in-betweens. If you have ever found a silent but compelling force deep within your being, calling you into a life of inner peace and joy, you have also experienced one of the little in-betweens found within the prayer-state called contemplation.

On the other hand, many people imagine themselves to have reached the exalted state of contemplation when they are still far removed from it. How can one know the difference between true contemplation and a false state of contemplation? Mainly by the fact that the people who imagine they have reached that state think they, themselves, entered into that state; when the truth of the matter is, no one, of himself, can *enter into* contemplation. The state of contemplation is a direct call and action of God which the person cannot bring to himself and must come from God.

True infused contemplation cannot be acquired or produced by the person even after a lifetime of faithful prayer. A person can use vocal prayer, mental prayer and meditation for many long years and still never once experience the wondrous sweetness and joys of true contemplation if *God does not call* the person into that state.

It would be better to describe contemplation as a spiritual experience or a direct call from God to the soul rather than call it a prayer. In true contemplation, there are no prayers in the same way that we pray to God with other forms of prayers. It is more the soul experiencing God's love in a way which could never be experienced simply by praying. It is truly a religious experience unlike any other. A person cannot even understand what that means unless he or she has actually experienced the feelings deep within the soul. Such information is very important to know, especially for the person who decides that he has already reached the contemplative stage of union with God, when in reality, he has no idea what contemplation is all about.

Many people who taste the first sweet fruits of a spiritual awakening, such as occur during a dramatic conversion, tend to accept that experience as the ultimate in union with God. They imagine that such an encounter automatically pushed them not only to the top of THE LADDER OF PERFECTION but into the prayer of contemplation as well. Such people are mistaken. The good Lord does not share His most intimate treasures found in the prayer of contemplation with souls not prepared to receive or understand such treasures.

Before a person can even hope for these treasures, he must, first of all, polish all other forms of prayers. He also must find a very great inner joy in praying to his beloved Lord.

The fleeting moments of contemplation which I have described are just that: fleeting. They are but a taste of what can be expected if one would preserve and not become discouraged in the quest for perfection. If a person makes the mistake of believing he has entered into contemplation, when he has not, he will end up "telling God" what he thinks God is "telling him." Then pride sets in and the person begins to believe that he is the only one on earth praying as a person should pray.

A false contemplative life is very dangerous and can destroy a person's whole union with God. Saint Teresa of Avila was very emphatic about that. She advised any nun, who was caught up in false contemplative mysticism, to eat and sleep more as a cure.

The prayer of contemplation is often divided into two sections. These are acquired contemplation and infused contemplation. Acquired contemplation is not actually contemplation at all, but a very high stage of mental prayer. Within this stage, the person still is in control of prayer. That is why it is called acquired. In all forms of prayer as in acquired contemplation, the human mind, will and intellect work responding to grace. But *it is the person who acts!* He reaches out to God through physical or mental activity. He is the one who is taking each and every slow, painful step up that LADDER OF PERFECTION. God is more or less on the side lines always ready to give the grace necessary for the climb, but it is the person who must of his own free will make the effort and "run the race."

The heart, mind and will reach out to God with the human element attached. The person must desire to pray or meditate and then pray or go to Mass or pull out the Rosary beads or the Novena booklet. These actions make the prayer life an "I" or "me" sort of activity. It must begin with the person's own motivation, aided by grace, to bring the action to fulfillment and fruition. Then when the action ends, the prayer ceases, the mental picture fades away, normal thoughts, ideas, dreams, hopes and temptations return. Very often the return of such thoughts bring sufferings and inner agony as life resumes its normal course.

At that point, one may begin to ask God "Why?" Why does such prayer bring joys and even consolations which all too quickly fade away once the prayer activity ceases? Even people who have advanced into high states of mental prayer, will wonder why God allows the soul to be doused with the cold waters of reality when one's whole being longs to taste only the sweetness of God's nearness and love found in prayer; especially, in the higher forms of prayer.

The answer is that the person's prayer is still encased in his own material, physical needs and so the person has not yet been able to abandon himself to a perfect (or near-perfect) trust in God's will for him. The person may still have traces of the "I want" which is the basic character of most lower forms of vocal prayers.

In other words, the person's prayer life may still be tarnished with the fault of attempting to tell God what He must do, instead of asking: "What *do you want me to do?*"

Very often that fault is well-hidden and unexposed but it is there. I have often discovered such a barrier in people who have left the early, lower forms of prayer and were well-advanced in their union with God. There remains the clinging to the deeply-embedded self-will which brings fears and anxieties about future life and living.

Christ told us not to be anxious and not to worry about what we wear or what we will eat, but people seldom pay any attention to His words. It is too difficult to follow His advice and too easy to fall victim to all sorts of daily worries and fears.

The fact is, one of the last human weaknesses which most people have on the rough journey to spiritual perfection is their lack of complete trust and faith in God's holy will for them. They can climb up the ladder to union with God, filled with love for Him, acquiring many virtues along the way and yet never really and truly trust God and His holy will with all the ups and downs of human existence. As a result, many of their prayers contain, with lesser or greater degrees, the requests or at least the desires to have God "do it their way" and not "His way."

Until a person learns how to trust God with his whole heart and soul, he or she will always feel that cold water chill away the sweetness and joy found in a very close union with God. When the person possesses this trust and faith, he or she will feel spiritual joys and peace *in spite* of the ups and downs of daily living. That is mainly the difference between the prayer of contemplation and the lower forms of prayer or the difference between acquired and infused contemplation.

When God calls a soul into infused contemplation, God alone acts. And the joys of that experience are lasting even when the experience ends. Why? Because as I said, true contemplation, the infused kind, becomes not just an isolated experience but a way of life.

What then, exactly, is infused contemplation and how would a person know that God has indeed called him or her into such a prayer experience?

Infused contemplation is what I call a "changeover" when God "reaches down" to draw a soul into a wondrous union with Him, into the "walls of interior silence and recollection."

Throughout the whole of a person's prayer life up to infused contemplation, there have been numerous struggles, spiritual battles, turmoils, temptations, distractions, etc. Then, suddenly, one glorious moment, the soul notes a remarkable change in the prayer life.

At a given moment, chosen only by God, with no knowledge of what is to happen, the person finds his or her soul surrounded by a peace which was never experienced before. This peace covers the soul like an ocean wave, but more, wraps the soul in a magnificent feeling of God's own presence and love. The years of spiritual struggle fade away and the soul can love God and feel

His love without one ounce of resistance or distraction or inter-ference. The soul throws itself, or rather, God pulls the soul into His arms of love.

There have been many names given to this type of a prayer experience. It has been called The Mystical Marriage, The Prayer of Full Union or The Prayer of Quiet. The soul passes into a super-natural state of union with the God who dwells deep within the soul. "The interior castle," as Saint Teresa of Avila calls it, at last comes into full view and the soul becomes completely united with the Divine Presence dwelling deep within that castle. God has captured the soul and the person, knows for sure, without one ounce of doubt that its goal has been reached: it is in complete union with God.

The person who emerges from this experience is not the same person who entered into such a union with God. Never again can life and living bring the same old worries, fears and anxieties. Daily crosses and sufferings are seen in the light of their true spir-itual value. Little, petty things in life which at one time seemed to be so important and occupied so much time and thought are now seen as "nothing." Daily duties and obligations are done with joy and far better than ever before. All virtues are strengthened and polished.

Now, please do not confuse this with one such as a "born again" experience. There is a vast difference between the two. A "born again" experience is the start of one's climb up THE LADDER OF PERFECTION. Infused contemplation and its results can be found *only near the very* top of the ladder after years of spiritual strug-gles and battles.

When one has been given the magnificent grace or blessing of infused contemplation, the soul is thrown into a delightful, pro-found awareness of being very close to God, but more: of under-standing the God whom it now knows exists in all His infinite love and mercy. A person may want to dance with joy and shout his gladness to the world; however, he does not.

Here is another difference between the "born again" experience and infused contemplation. The "born again" Christians shout from the roof tops their joy and praises of the Lord. They do indeed tell the whole world about their "finding" the Lord. Their actions and words, which may be a sign of their love for the Lord whom they have discovered, actually are more of a sign of their spiritual immaturity. They act as little children do, singing and dancing, shouting and publicly displaying their emotions. Far too often they remain on that low level of spirituality, never growing, never maturing, always content with their childish ways and understanding of their personal relationship with God.

Of course, it can be said that the type of spirituality they display is better than none at all. However, the search for union with the God whom a person has discovered must never become a placid, stagnant happening. Climbing THE LADDER OF PERFECTION is just that: climbing. There is a constant spiritual growth, a constant reaching out to touch the one who has captured the heart. There are the unending spiritual battles, the falls, the risings, the defeats, the triumphs! It is a great mistake for a person to place limits upon his spiritual life, such as often happens among the "born again" Christians. Once I witnessed a meeting of such Christians and I was amazed to learn that the group had been in existence for six years. In spite of the six years, they sang the same songs, shouted the same praises to the Lord and read the same Bible passages without any apparent spiritual growth.

If there had been spiritual growth, they would have very quickly sought their union with God with less noise and more silence.

Because infused contemplation can come only after the weary climb step by step up the ladder, when the soul finally rests in that blissful state, there must, of necessity, be a silent encounter with the Lord. Such an experience is so precious, so profound, so filled with awe and wonderment that the person would never want to talk about or even attempt to describe it for fear of losing the aura of its memory. For, as I often said, in order to find the God who dwells within the soul and have union with that God, a person must, first of all, find the silence wherein He dwells.

The stilling of the mind, interior mortification, getting rid of distractions, praying in a silent place are all a must if a person is ever to understand and possess the silence needed for God's call into the interior castle of infused contemplation.

Chapter 7

THOSE WHO ARE READY
FOR CONTEMPLATION

Because infused contemplation can only come as a gift from God and because this gift is bestowed upon very few souls, a person can only prepare his soul for such a call and not actually enter this state by and through his own power. Very often, even souls which have been living on a very high level of spirituality never receive this call from God. That does not, in any way, decrease their holiness. Nor, on the other hand, does infused contemplation make saints what they are. As I said, saints are made by and through the ordinary way and means of sanctification. And infused contemplation is not an ordinary means of sanctification.

Very often, favored contemplative souls, who spend long hours lost in prayer are not welcomed in active religious communities for they might disrupt normal daily routines. One has only to read the lives of saints who were carried away in holy ecstasies or raptures for days at a time to understand why.

Many contemplatives become so engrossed in the joys and peace found in contemplation that they tend to forget the fact that they live in a normal, active world filled with millions of people who have millions of daily problems. They want to withdraw into their own private union with God. That is one reason why a person in the world cannot enjoy the state of infused contemplation as can a contemplative Trappist monk who spends five or six hours in daily silent prayer with the rest of his community.

Yet, in spite of that drawback, a lay person can be called by God into periods of deep, infused contemplation. The length of the prayer time must of necessity be shortened due to pressing daily duties; however, the intensity of the encounter with Christ can be just as profound. Also, it is possible for a highly contemplative soul who lives among the distractions of the world to enter into, what I call, the final prayer stage of Holy Abandonment. When that happens, the person finds his spiritual fulfillment in bringing the joys and peace of the contemplative life with him no matter where he goes or what he does. The person, also by that time has learned that what is lacking because of less time for prayer is found in more time for charity. When a person is called into infused contemplation, there is also infused into the soul overpowering desires to be, at all times, "alone with the alone." That, as I said, is not possible for the average lay person, so the contemplative, instead of retreating from the world and people, *brings* the fruits of his or her own personal union with God to the world and people by and through numerous acts of charity and brotherly love. The fact is, it is said, that contemplative prayer without charity is no prayer at all.

Now, when would a person be ready for the sublime state of infused contemplation? Of course, the final plunge into that state is completely in the hands of God, so just because a person may deem himself or herself ready for that encounter, there is no guarantee that it will happen. However, it should definitely be the goal for anyone who wants to climb THE LADDER OF PERFECTION to a close union with God. Infused contemplation is, without a doubt, the "pearl of great value" which we all should strive to own. It should never fade away, it should always be there before the eyes of our souls, ever encouraging us to keep climbing no matter how many falls or slips occur during the struggle. The rewards are worth all the struggles and spiritual battles.

The fact is, all the struggles, battles and slips are necessary if one is to reach the state wherein infused contemplation can occur. These spiritual crosses and sufferings help to prepare the soul by purifying it for that state.

Infused contemplation is the state wherein the soul's attention is fixed upon God in such a way that God reveals to the soul profound secrets of His love. The soul's knowledge about and understanding of God is expanded as the love between God and the soul grows. However, God does not reveal the deepest secrets of His divine Heart to just anyone, nor does He grant the state of infused contemplation to just anyone. A soul must be purified in a very exacting manner if the soul could ever hope to enjoy the sweetness of so intimate a union with Him. God purges and purifies a soul in order to bring it into the condition necessary for His wondrous gift of infused contemplation. The person must not only allow such a purification by accepting and loving God's holy will but must also cooperate with the graces sent by God which are needed to overcome sins, weaknesses and faults and acquire great virtue.

I am not saying that you must become a living saint before you could be called into infused contemplation. But I will say that most people who were called into that state were indeed saints. The greatest contemplatives of all time were saints who knew how to first do penance and pray. Still, there is hope for an ordinary lay person to enjoy the same fruits of infused contemplation which these great saints enjoyed but not without the preparation needed.

Now, say that after a long climb up THE LADDER OF PERFECTION, both you and your spiritual director begin to look for signs that point you towards infused contemplation, what would these signs be?

First of all, never judge for yourself these signs. That would be very dangerous and could actually destroy your whole prayer life and union with God which you have worked so hard to achieve. Some of the signs which are used to tell if a person is ready for infused contemplation will show up in lower forms of prayer. Only a competent spiritual director can understand such signs. Such a director, who has guided a soul up THE LADDER OF PERFECTION for a number of years, or who, at least, knows what the person is striving for must examine these signs from all angles because they could be most deceptive. It is wise to follow a director's advice and not to attempt to decide for oneself if the soul is ready for a call into infused contemplation.

One of the first signs to be considered by such a director would be the person's increasing desires for the deep, spiritual silence necessary for infused contemplation. This desire is far different and more profound than what occurs during other prayer stages. It is also not an ordinary human need for a "bit of peace and quiet" in one's daily life. Many people who rush around a noisy life each day naturally long for moments of silence such as when all the children are finally sound asleep in bed. Also, some people develop a severe emotional problem wherein they want to withdraw from the realities of life into a silent world apart from life's daily duties and obligations. That is not the type of desires for silence I am talking about.

The desires for silence which come near the top of the ladder or in the highest prayer stages are deeply and profoundly felt; so much so, that ordinary noises and material distractions actually cause the person a deep inner pain and suffering. The person would want to run away, as soon as possible, from such noises because they interfere with the soft, gentle love song which is sung between the soul and the God who dwells deep within that soul.

At this point in the person's spiritual development, this song has slowly but surely emerged from the depths of the person's soul. However, it is still so soft and fragile that the slightest wrong move or noise could make it quickly disappear.

That is one of the differences between a soul called into infused contemplation and a soul still not ready or preparing for such a call. After God draws the soul into the state of infused contemplation, the love song sung between the soul and the Divine Presence is so loud, so clear, so strong and so in tune that nothing can destroy it nor keep it from reaching the ears of the person's soul which had been drawn into that state. Truly a soul which is living a life of infused contemplation actually shares the joys of heaven which come from hearing the sweet, melodious songs of love originating from the Sacred Heart of Christ.

The desires for silence, which I am talking about, wrap themselves around the soul like a warm blanket which attempts to protect the soul from the coldness of noise and material distractions. The person begins to want to escape from these distractions; even the ones which had at one time been so much a part of the person's daily life. Many things which the person loved to do a year before or even months before become now sources of discomfort for the soul and they begin to lose their appealing, attractive nature. The loud music on the radio, the exciting T.V. shows, the bowling dates, the golf games, the useless conversations, the gossip, the hours spent on useless hobbies and so forth, suddenly become meaningless as the ears of the soul strain to catch a note of that love song sung between itself and Christ.

Another sign equally as important as these desires for silence is the person's desires to do penance for his or her sins. A person cannot even hope to enter into infused contemplation unless and until he admits his own sinfulness and finds the way, through penance as well as through prayer, to make amends. The person will find a new love in his heart for the sacrament of penance (confession) and will find tremendous joy when the priest says: "I absolve you from all your sins." Then he will leave the room, where his confession took place, filled with a longing to do penance for his sins. These acts of penance need not be difficult, harsh nor public. They can constitute little acts during the day such as doing a little job the person hates to do with a love for God's holy will as an act of penance. The person can express a kind word to someone he dislikes, as an act of penance for his sins. There are numerous, hidden ways to do penance. Sometimes just getting out of bed to go to work can become an act of penance.

These acts of penance not only help prepare the soul for infused contemplation but also act as a barrier to stave off the devastating effects of a too-guilty, scrupulous conscience.

Another sign which indicates that a person may be ready for a call into infused contemplation is the person's withdrawing his love and affection from material pleasures, objects or even persons who may lead the soul away from its goals of a more complete union with God.

I am, of course, not talking about withdrawing the love and affection which a person has for members of his family or for close, dear friends. The fact is, when the person's love is less divided among pleasures, objects and persons not on the same spiritual path, the person's love for members of his family and dearest friends will increase.

Also, the person's general love for others will increase as charity is polished and practiced.

We all know (or at least we have heard about) the fellow who has made his wife a "bowling widow" or a "golf widow," or who will spend hours with his "buddies" away from his wife and children playing cards or in a tavern drinking beer. We all know of people who will love material objects to excess while, at the same time, care little about the important things in life.

When a person has reached the prayer state of being called into infused contemplation, all these types of loves and affections will slowly, but surely fade away. That is the spiritual result of desiring to gather up all these wasted loves and affections so that the person can have more love and affection to offer to Christ. Christ told us we cannot serve two masters and we also cannot divide our love and affection into a "million" pieces and then expect to "love" Christ with our whole heart, mind and will.

A person who prepares for the call into infused contemplation must, of necessity, prepare his heart by emptying it of all useless loves and affections which taint and spoil the purity of the love which the person wants to offer to Christ.

Along with that sign, there is the one of being unable to meditate as before. This is a very tricky sign and must be handled with much caution. There are many reasons why a person can have problems meditating. That does not, mean that he is ready for infused contemplation.

What I am talking about, as the sign indicating that a person is ready for that sublime state, is a certain restlessness which the soul experiences during periods of intense meditation. Up to that point, the person has found much joy and sweetness in this type of prayer. Suddenly, the soul seems to be surrounded by aridities which have no reason and cannot be explained. The sweet conversations with the Lord seem to be "stale" or stagnant unable to bring joy to the soul.

The first reaction is the person taking upon himself the blame, declaring that he must have done something "terrible" and the Lord is angry. The truth of the matter is that the person has outgrown that state of prayer and is ready for an advancement into a more mature state: infused contemplation.

Now, in order to be more sure that the person has prepared his or her soul for the call into infused contemplation, theologians tell us that all the signs must be present at one time. The person must have great desires or longings for the silence wherein Christ dwells, he must have desires to do penance for his sins to further purify his soul, he must feel that he should withdraw his love and affection from all unnecessary pleasures and time-consuming occupations or hobbies, he has a feeling that his meditation has lost its spiritual satisfaction.

One final sign which I believe is conclusive evidence that the person is ready for a call into infused contemplation is the fact that when the person wants to pray, his prayer becomes mainly a silent prayer. The soul wants to just rest without words spoken. The memory, the understanding, the will, the mind are completely at rest in a profound, beautiful state of aloneness. In this state, only one thing is present: love. The soul loves God and is loved by Him. There is no need for words or mental pictures or remembrances. The soul explodes with love and joy and yet cannot really understand where all the love and joy come from. The soul finds no spiritual battles, no conflicts, just tremendous peace and quiet as the soul gives its full and complete attention to the God who dwells deep within the soul.

This does not mean that the person sits all day in a silent Church or room and falls into a trance. There is no trace of false mysticism in what I am talking about; although, there could develop such so it is imperative that the proper spiritual direction is given. The state I am talking about could last only a moment and usually does at the beginning of this type of spiritual experience. Or the state could last for one half an hour. I would become very suspicious if it lasts longer than one half an hour especially if the person has not as yet entered into a contemplative way of life. For, the average person cannot tarry longer than that with so many daily duties and responsibilities to attend to.

At first, the breaking away from so sweet and precious a prayer state will be most painful. However, the pain will becomes less and less and can eventually disappear once the person is skilled in this method of prayer. Also, always remember that no matter how far advanced a person's prayer life becomes, he should never give up the lower forms of prayer such as vocal prayer or even mental prayers. In other words, the prayer life should be complete and diversified.

Now, even if the person has reached the state of being ready for infused contemplation, that does not mean that God will call the soul into such a lofty state.

As I said, infused contemplation can only be obtained by God calling the soul to such lofty heights; and He seldom does that.

Yet, do not becomes discouraged if your soul does not receive such a call. There remains the state called acquired contemplation. That state in itself is a most wondrous prayer stage to be in; and is an advanced prayer state all by itself. By having your soul pass through all the signs of being ready for God's call into infused contemplation, you will have reached the acquired state of contemplation and there are numerous joys and sweetness to be found there. So don't even try to have God call you into infused contemplation. The acquired contemplation can bring you into a most loving union with God.

PART TWO

THE PRAYER LIFE OF
HOLY ABANDONMENT

Chapter 1

THE PERFECTION OF HOLY ABANDONMENT

The spiritual term, abandonment to God's holy will, becomes the name for a very close union with God. It becomes part of the prayer of contemplation inasmuch as it depends upon and demands a special grace from God. One could not even begin the practice of this lofty stage of prayer without this gift. However, when one reaches this spiritual height and receives this gift, it becomes fairly easy to follow this state of Holy Abandonment. The word easy is not really correct. What should be said is that the person becomes so used to completely conforming himself or herself to the will of God that there is no need for any effort or struggle to do that. A good way to tell that such a state has not been reached is to find out how much effort or pain is felt when a cross is placed upon one's shoulder or if something is desired which may cast a shadow upon the glow of union with God.

There is a saying in the spiritual life which goes something like this: "follow the Lamb wherever He goes." That is exactly what Holy Abandonment is all about. It is to follow His lead, His examples, His virtues as you walk through the tangle of daily duties and obligations. Most people cannot do that simply because they bump into their own self-interests, self-love or self-desires. In a simple sentence, Holy Abandonment is to do everything for and with God, to think only the way God would think in your place, to desire only what would be best for your soul and to accept all the lights and shadows of God's actions in your life.

It is *not* to become totally consumed by religion so that all material things, including duties and obligations, fade from view. It *is* to be totally consumed by your love for God's holy will as you go through life doing only what He wants you to do. It is to become a channel of His grace so that He can use you, turn you around, shape your life only as He wants to without one ounce of resistance on your part. Not only that but your interior, hidden self must remain in a state of total oneness with God so that you allow your soul to sing an uninterrupted song of pure love to Him no matter what happens in your material life. Holy Abandonment is an interior (not so much exterior) renunciation of all things in the world which could distract you from the object of your affection. In other words, you still must live in the world among worldly people, among material things, with daily conflicts, arguments, etc. However, if you have reached the state of true Holy Abandonment nothing which happens in your material life will distract you from the pure love union with God who dwells within your soul. You then not only have God dwelling within your soul but you see Him there, are aware of His presence and join Him and love Him every moment of every day and night.

How is it possible for anyone to reach such lofty heights? It is possible through grace. It is also possible because you, a child of God, are capable of imitating Him. Christ taught us to be perfect as our heavenly Father is perfect. If Christ said that then there has to be a way to this perfection and a means to obtain it.

Before I continue with explaining more about Holy Abandonment, let me explain a bit about perfection, that perfection of God's which Christ told us to gather unto ourselves (*Matthew* 5:48).

When God gives us the grace which is needed and becomes the means of obtaining perfection or perfect union with God, this grace causes us to be so combined with God, as Father and child, that we then become capable of being like the Father. In other words, we actually share His nature through grace. We become one with God as St. Paul teaches. It is God who lives in us: "...put on the new nature, created after the likeness of God in true righteousness and holiness" (*Ephesians* 4:24). That being the case, we now can share in God's own perfection. Saint Thomas Aquinas tells us that each person is perfect in the way in which the person participates in the divine perfection. In addition, our perfection, or the state of perfection which God wants us to reach, has already been deeply embedded in the infinite mind of God. When we reach this perfection, we then reflect this image of God's perfection which He created us to reflect. If we do not reach this perfection, then we cannot become what God created us to become.

In order to better understand what is meant by such teachings, compare a quest for perfection to a talent given to a great artist such as Michelangelo.

St. Thomas Aquinas teaches that God alone, as the Creator, becomes the cause of man's creations. Everything man builds or creates, that is good, stems from the infinite mind of God, who makes man the agent to bring His ideas into view.

For example, it can be safely assumed that in Heaven there existed the original of all mankind's greatest works of art which inspire and bring spiritual joy to the viewers. The statues, paintings, Churches, music and such were already created in Heaven or were an idea of God's before an agent of His on earth acted to reproduce the work of art. Surely the Holy Scriptures were created in Heaven, in the infinite mind of God, long before they were written on earth.

Saint Thomas teaches that all that exists has its being from God. Ideas exist in God's mind in the shape of models which can be copied by man because of man's relationship to God which He created to be one of imitation: man being the imitator.

St. Thomas further teaches that although created things such as great works of art, receive the driving force, which places them into a state of existence more or less independently of God, the Creator, they receive a second impulse which leads them back to their starting place causing them to return to the source from where the idea originated.

In other words, no artist or creator of objects on earth, can claim for himself the credit for his own works. Such credit belongs only to God, form where he received the idea or model, by way of inspiration, to create. Also he carried out what he thought were his own ideas by way and means of the talent which was also from God.

If one were to think deeply about this truth, one would realize that such has to be so because not only is a talent a gift from God but also are the things used by man to bring into existence his own works; such as, stone, wood, clay, dyes, etc.

Art is a creation or depiction of Christian themes in visual form, the painting, statue, writing, can bring to man praises and glory. However, from where did the theme or ideas emerge? Where did the inspiration originate? Where did the model exist before it existed in the mind of the talented artist or writer?

Does man have the inborn power to create solely with his own ideas and talents or must he admit that in himself he is nothing? Being nothing, having nothing, how can he create what was nothing from the beginning? The answer can only be that man imitates what was already created in the being and mind of God.

God allows this and also allows the arts and sciences freedom in their own spheres to use their own principles and methods. By his arts and technological skills and talents, man has wonderfully transformed the material world (or at least part of it) into the image God had in His infinite mind before earth was created. Man may then seem to be the master of the world because he does possess the ability to transform it into a reality of beauty, through art, and progress, through science; however, not one idea or creation stemmed from his own intellect. For his very intelligence is but a reflection of God's. Whatever he possesses as a person, all his capabilities are not his, because he remains a nothing created from a nothing. Man was indeed created from a nothing. However, he was, in a very positive way, created as a mirror to reflect the sublime abilities of the Creator; so he becomes a something but only as this mirror which captures the reflection of God and His ways and ideas.

In much the same way, earth was created as a mirror to reflect the grandeurs of Heaven. Thus we had the perfect Garden of Eden where there was order, peace and no decay or death. Some theologians teach that the Garden of Eden did not really exist as a garden but merely as a state of existence achieved only through sanctifying grace which brought our first parents in union with

God. However, if such an explanation were true, then everyone whose soul is in the state of grace would be living in Eden. We all know that even if our souls are in the state of grace, we do not live in a paradise called Eden. If man was created, and he was, to become a living mirror which would be used by God to capture His ways, ideas and perfection, then this mirror had to be placed in an Eden which reflected the beauties and order of Heaven; otherwise, the wonders of His creations would have had defects and God could not create flaws. God created in perfection with perfection and desired perfection for His children and their world. Both the world and man were devoid of self-perfection. They received their perfection only from the touch of God.

However, man was also given a precious gift called free will. It can be assumed that the first man and woman understood the state of perfection which they were in. They also understood the way they were only a mirror reflecting some degree of God's holiness. If they did not understand this, they could not have lost grace. Because they used their free will to choose sin, they understood the difference between perfection and sin. But, even so, they fell.

By falling, our first parents shattered not only their own mirror, but the mirror of earth as well. As a result, the reflections of God the Creator were distorted. So mankind was left with fallen human nature and a world filled with much decay and barren wastelands.

Still, God, in His infinite mercy and love for His children, desired the union with them which was now lost. He wanted man and woman to become much more than a distorted reflection of what He was. He wanted His grace and holiness reflected in their souls. He wanted His ideas of beauty and achievements to reflect within the deeds and work of His children. He wanted His world, His earth to develop as man and woman use the talents which He would give to them.

However, man in himself (and woman in herself) had nothing to offer to God for his own salvation or restoration except a distorted reflection of His own goodness, holiness and perfection.

God then sent His only-begotten Son, Christ, as an offering to

Himself, as the sacrifice needed to bind the broken tie between God and man. God, in that way, restored the mirror of mankind so man could once more become the imitator of His ways and perfection and the image of His goodness and virtue.

It is interesting to note that most of the greatest artistic and scientific achievements of mankind were brought into the world only after the death of Christ. So also were the greatest men and women who could be called saints. The greatest person of all, Mary, whose grace far outshone Eve's, was sanctified through the anticipated merits of Christ her Son. No other human being reflected as great a portion of God's perfection as did Mary. As she said herself: "My soul magnifies the Lord" (*Luke* 1:46). The mirror of her soul was never broken or shattered.

There were, of course, great works of art and even scientific accomplishments of man before the birth and death of Christ. However, compare the magnificent religious artistries and modern scientific wonders to the art and inventions of ancient pagans. What was produced before the time of Christ was only a tiny fragment of what man could accomplish or do, no matter how grand and noble were the deeds and works of mankind before the Redemption. Why? Because such works were created using the reflection of God's ideas which could be seen only through the pieces of a broken mirror. What was seen by pagans and what they attempted to imitate was only a vague, fogged image of the one true God and His works.

Note also the fact that the only worship of the one true God, before the time of Christ, came from the Jewish people to whom God made a personal covenant, cementing together some of the broken pieces, as a preparation for the coming of Christ.

After the Redemption, the mirror needed to reflect God's ways, deeds and ideas was completely restored to its former state. Man could now reach the union of perfection which God wanted him to reach; however, man still retained his free will. Man had the power of grace to keep the mirror of his soul intact but, he also had the same free will which Adam and Eve used to shatter that first mirror. Yet, now there was a vast difference between these two similarities. The differential being the fact that when

Adam and Eve shattered the mirror used by God to reflect His image into the mind and soul of man, the only one who could repair the damage was Christ. After the Redemption it was man, himself, who had the ability to repair his own mirror no matter how often it is broken and shattered. How was that possible?

It was made possible because man now had the magnificent gift of grace *within the control of his own free will*! By his use of grace, he could use his free will to accept and to respond to the fruits of salvation brought upon mankind through the death of Christ. It is interesting to note that Saint Paul called man a slave before the Redemption. After the death of Christ, we became the children of God. "See what love the Father has given us, that we should be called the children of God; and so we are" (*1 John* 3:1). As children of God, we now can receive the mercy and forgiveness of a loving Father individually.

Yet, we still must struggle to reach a perfect union with that Father. Remember that Christ's death and the stream of grace which was poured down upon man and woman guarantees final victory or salvation; but it *does not* guarantee that all men would accept and respond to such grace. There could be no guarantee of that because if there were, man would, of necessity, lose his free will. God always must have a way to ask each and every person He ever created the very same question He asked the angels and Adam and Eve: "Will you follow me?" He never said: "I command you to follow me regardless of whether you want to or do not want to." Christ said: "If a man loves me, he will keep my word and my Father will love him and We will come to him and make our home with him" (*John* 14:23). Note the word "if." Christ did not say: "Everyone will love me even if they do not want to love me." It is our own choice, to follow God and His ways, which brings forth to us the wondrous fruits of our own salvation. That being the case, it is also our own choice to keep in perfect shape the mirror within our souls or to shatter it through sin. Man has the option: to imitate God, His ways and His deeds or to lose sight of God, His ways and His deeds by destroying the mirror used to reflect them in our souls.

Now it can be understood why a sinner, who has lost grace, has such distorted, twisted ideas about God and His ways. How such a person rants and rages about God, tearing His divine image apart! He can do that because he destroyed the mirror in his own soul (mirror is another word for grace) and can no longer see a clear reflection of God. Christ also said: "If you love me (note the "if" again), keep my commandments" (*John* 14:15). To keep the commandments of God, which include the commandments and teachings of the Church is to show God how much a person really loves Him. However, in order to keep the commandments and to love God, this person must, first of all, know and understand the God who gave him these laws to obey. Knowledge and understanding are two gifts of the Holy Spirit which come when the mirror in the soul remains unbroken. By and through these two gifts, man is better able to see and respond to the image or reflection of God which is within the mirror in his soul.

Once this mirror is broken, once grace flees the soul by way of mortal sin, it is almost impossible to know and to understand the God who gave us the commandments. Under such circumstances it is also almost impossible to love God and it is impossible to become perfect as God in Heaven is perfect.

Then, as long as the mirror remains broken, as long as the soul is without grace, the person exists with a broken, distorted reflection of God within his or her soul. Once the image of God is so distorted, once a man cannot see a clear image of God so as to be able to imitate His ways of perfection, the person can more clearly see the reflection of the devil and his ways. Then when man creates, he can easily build up works of the devil instead of works of God. The devil can and does guide and lead man away from the ways and ideas of God. The devil can, in this way, cause man to imitate his evil and disobedience.

It is most interesting to note that among Pagan religions of the past and present, there is much devil worship. Pagan men often carve or paint devil images instead of images of the one true God. After the Redemption, man began to paint pictures of the one true God and of Mary, the Mother of God and to create beautiful statues of the same.

Grace then becomes the channel or mirror used by God to

project His image, ways and perfection into His creatures called man. Saint Thomas tells us that creatures (men) have no goodness or perfection which they can consider their own. All begins with the creator who made man for the purpose of imitating His own perfection.

So, that being the case, it is indeed possible to reach the state of perfection which Christ calls us to reach; because it is possible for man to imitate God the Father who sends us the grace which is needed to so imitate Himself.

Saint Thomas also tells us that God leaves no man untouched by His influence. However, to be touched by the influence of God is one thing; to use free will to carry out this touch of grace is another thing.

So, if a person wishes to reach the very heights of prayer called Holy Abandonment, he must freely accept the graces which will enable him to imitate God's ways and virtues. There must be a free abandonment of oneself in favor of imitating the perfection of God; because Holy Abandonment at all times means: what do you, dear God, want me to do now? Then this abandonment must be carried into: what do you, dear God, want me to believe? Finally: I love your holy will, do with me as you so desire.

If one does reach this sublime state of prayer, one will discover the perfect harmony between one's own will and God's will. The sweet music of agreement will permeate every action, thought, word or deed. Doubts, fears and confusion about God, life and living will completely disappear. The person will not even think of doing one tiny thing which will displease God. All purely, worldly human desires will slowly fade into the background and disappear for the person will know that he has all he needs for perfect peace, joy and happiness. Nothing on earth, not even a human love, can bring the sweet, tender joys of such a holy, pure union with God.

Again, how can one actually reach the heights of prayer wherein Holy Abandonment takes place? The climb upward is arduous, long and often it seems impossible.

As with all spiritual advancement, the first step to take is to do all in your power to forget your own interests and desires and to replace them with God's. Now, before you can even attempt to do that, such a spiritual state must be clearly understood. A misunderstanding can cause havoc with one's spiritual life. A friend of mine told me she was petrified to even attempt such an abandonment to God's holy will because she thought it meant giving up her own free will and turning into a robot.

The first question to ask toward an understanding of the state of Holy Abandonment is: what is God's will for me if I forget my own interests and desires? The answer will surprise you. It is God's will for you to continue your daily life, (if the life is filled with His grace; if not, then the first step will be to change a life of sin into a life of grace) to accept all your duties and responsibilities and the many crosses and sufferings which manage to sneak into 24 hours of daily living. In other words, you do not have to leave your state of life to find Holy Abandonment.

Nor do you give up your free will. You will still be free to plan to improve your state of life, to build a new home, buy things, get a job advancement, etc. But, as you carry out such plans (or try to) as you faithfully fulfill the duties and obligations of your daily life, you learn how to share your daily life with God and to do things only to please Him. What will displease Him? Well, sin for one thing. Not overcoming sins, faults and weaknesses and acquiring virtue will displease Him. Blaming Him for all the ills of your life, will surely not please Him; so will not obeying His laws and the laws of His Church.

It is the sharing of everything in your life: that is of uppermost importance. Because when God, His grace and virtue enter the picture, you *will* plan and desire *nothing* that can in any way hurt grace or virtue or God's goodness.

Such a spiritual state is definitely not one of turning into a robot with no human will. Some Oriental mysticisms do reduce their followers to a state of see not, hear not, think not and speak not. But that is not Holy Abandonment. That is attempting to destroy a person's free will. The difference between the true Holy Abandonment of our Catholic religion and the false mysticism of some other religions is that with our religion the person's free will not only remains intact, but is absolutely necessary in order to live the life of the prayer of abandonment. The free will must come forth to choose the elements necessary to live this abandonment. Holy Abandonment is *not* no longer caring about what happens in your daily life, as would be found in a morbid state of mental and spiritual inactivity, but in using free will to make sure that this daily life is lived within the sunshine of God's love and grace.

Activity abounds within the wondrous state of Holy Abandonment. In desiring to please God, the person must constantly use his free will to avoid sin and acquire virtue, to obey the laws and rules of God and of His Church, to use grace, to increase moments of prayer, meditation, spiritual reading, charity and such.

Not only that but there is a constant desire to keep in motion the wondrous activity between the soul and its divine guest by anticipating what will please this guest the most and then carrying out good intentions.

Holy Abandonment is regulating your whole life only according to your desires to please God as you carry out the duties and responsibilities of your daily life. It is to conform your will with God's will for you by becoming a better, a more spiritual person. It is to make your will and God's will into one so that if you were to say to him: "Your will is mine," He could quickly reply: "Your will is mine."

Holy Abandonment is to allow God to shape your whole being into a magnificent image of His own perfection with not one ounce of resistance on your part. In other words, it is to live in the fullest the very fist commandment of God: "You are to love God with your whole heart, your whole mind, your whole soul" (*Matthew* 22:37).

Very, very few people actually taste the divine fruits of such a union with God simply because they will not allow God to be first in their lives and to shape their beings as He so desires.

In order to reach the heights of the prayer of Holy Abandonment, a person must allow God to enter into his daily life with His grace; because the final stages of this spiritual state can come only through the direct action of God upon the soul.

However, God cannot act in this manner unless the person freely chooses to allow God to so act.

How is this done? As I stated in other chapters, the person must, first of all, use grace to overcome sins, faults and weaknesses. Then the person must become so accustomed to virtue, doing only what pleases God, that this way of life becomes a habit. Then after all that is done, the person moves into inner virtues of purifying his love for God. That brings him into the state of accomplishing heroic acts of virtue. It is within the realm of producing heroic acts of virtue where you find the canonized saints. Why? Because as difficult as it is to overcome sins, faults and weaknesses and to acquire and polish virtues, that is only the beginning of all which can be accomplished in the spiritual life. To do that makes a great amount of grace; however, it is the person using this grace which brings him or her into sight of the higher levels of holiness. But when the soul advances to the higher levels, then it is God who calls the soul to these heights. The person can do no more to increase his or her own holiness beyond a certain point. Holy Abandonment calls for God to draw the soul to Himself into a much closer union with Him. It is God who shapes the soul into what He wants it to become as long as the person allows God to do that.

What does that mean, to allow God to come forth to shape one's soul into what He wants it to become? It means to allow God to bestow upon you extraordinary gifts and graces. Some of these gifts and graces can be visions or great missions to accomplish for God; however, changes are they will not be, so please do not ask for such things desire them or think you possess them when you do not. Visions and great missions have nothing to do with personal sanctity. Even the saints, who did see visions, still had to purify their souls with the ordinary means of sanctification. They gained their sainthood through responding to grace and obedience, not in responding to visions. All the visions in the world could never had made them saints if they had not also found personal holiness by using grace and the sacraments and prayer.

Chapter 2

HEROIC ACTS OF VIRTUE

How do you allow God to bestow upon your soul extraordinary gifts and blessings? It is mainly by using the ordinary gifts He gives to you and accepting the graces which will help you become a holier person. The good Lord will never call you into the highest levels of union with Him if you have become abusive to the lower levels of grace and union with Him. If you have made it a habit to ignore, cast aside or reject the graces he pours upon your soul which will enable you to overcome sins, faults and weaknesses and to acquire virtue, then He and His graces will become more hidden in your daily life. He will not expose Himself and His presence more openly in your daily life if you have not prepared your soul to receive such a precious gift from Him. You prepare your soul by accepting and using all things: graces, sufferings, work, etc. for the good of your own soul and to help the souls of others. You prepare your soul by doing penance, mortification, making sacrifices so as to rid yourself of your own sins, faults and human weaknesses. Only then can the person reach the heights of holiness wherein God acts directly to lift him or her up to greater heights of union with Him. Then, and only then, can the soul lie within the stillness and quietude of the liberation from sins, faults, weaknesses and distractions of the world. Only then does the soul have the ability to sweetly say to its divine guest: "Draw me yet closer to your heart of love for I long to taste the wondrous joys which can be found there." Only then will God reveal more and more of His love and presence to the soul. Only then can He shape the soul into His desired image of His own perfection. Only then can the person start to perform heroic acts.

What are heroic acts? Well, they are seen in the lives of the saints. For example, Saint Bernadette spent many years in a convent where she was ignored and bound by a stern command never to mention her visions; even though, the other sisters were allowed to discuss all the latest news from Lourdes. Yet the saint found great joy within her life as a nun in spite of such sufferings. She practiced heroic acts of obedience. So did Saint Margaret Mary who was placed under the same type of obedience concerning the visions of the Sacred Heart. Saint Anthony practiced heroic acts of love for God and for souls when he went into a bee's nest of heresy and attempted to bring the truths of God to the people involved who did not welcome him or his message. By his determination and perseverance he did succeed in converting them. St. Teresa of Avila was ill most of her life; yet, in spite of all she suffered she was able to reform her religious order and to write important spiritual books. She performed heroic acts of virtue.

Now, what about your own heroic acts of virtue. What would be some examples of extraordinary acts of virtue in your own daily life done for the pure love of God? First, let me explain what are *not* heroic acts of virtue. Well, just going to Mass once a week, saying daily prayers, overcoming faults and sins, taking care of your daily duties, offering a helping hand to a friend in need, all such acts are not heroic. Why not? Because they are merely fulfilling your daily and religious duties and obligations. These are things which you, as a good Catholic, should be doing even if you have no desires to reach a closer union with God. I will also add here that going to special prayer meetings, getting all the so-called gifts of the Holy Spirit, putting them on public display, that also is *not* practicing heroic acts of virtue. Why do I say that these acts which may seem very special to some people are not heroic acts of virtue? Because they are not a solid foundation upon which to build a spiritual life. They can so easily lead away from God because of the development of human pride. The public display is what is so bad about them. The true virtue or gift of the prayer of Holy Abandonment is always a very personal, private, silent gift that one does not want others to notice or to share by talking about it. It is deeply rooted in a very pure humility which makes the gift very precious and very much in need of protection from eyes which have no right to view the wonders God works deep within the soul.

What then would be heroic acts of virtue in a plain, ordinary daily life of a lay person? A good sign that shows you that you are capable of performing heroic acts of virtue is to be able to look up at God, with tears streaming down your face, to smile and say: "Dearest God, I don't mind, I so love your holy will." Still, that may not be a heroic act because, as good Catholics, we should be able to do that just from the graces received from the sacraments and daily prayer. However, it is a sign that you are at least willing to go into the prayer of Holy Abandonment wherein heroic acts become second nature.

Heroic acts of virtue become then acts of goodness and holiness which go beyond the general requirements of living an active spiritual life or fulfilling religious and daily duties and obligations. Also, this "going beyond" must involve a great deal of humility and self-sacrifice. Each virtue which you do possess must be used at all times; but more, must be polished with a very pure love for God and His holy will.

For example: the virtues of love for God, faith, hope and charity must be practiced beyond the ordinary use of such virtues. How is that done, how can a person turn an ordinary virtue into a heroic act of virtue?

Let us look at the virtue of faith, which contains the virtues of humility and obedience. It is not too difficult, with the use of God's graces, to be a good or even an excellent Catholic believing all the Church teaches and obeying all laws and rules, until a law or rule tells you *not* to do what you want to do! Could you, under such circumstances, submit yourself to divine revelation, or to the laws of the Church and the infallibility of the Pope and give up your own plans? If you are divorced, and your first marriage was valid, and you want to remarry, could you change such plans knowing that the Church and God forbid the remarriage of such a person? If you could, then you are practicing a heroic act of virtue of faith. However, many of such Catholics fail such a test of faith and obedience because they never reached the heights of union with God wherein lies the ability to practice heroic acts of virtue.

Most Catholics, I dare say 90 per cent of Catholics, will never and could never practice heroic acts of virtue simply because they never made their prayer lives advance toward closer union with God. As a result, they never prepared their souls the correct way so that God could rise them into the realm of union wherein the person has the ability to practice heroic virtues.

Such a lack of ability to practice heroic acts of virtue is constantly seen within the lives of lay people. I am really amazed to discover a Catholic, who for years has gone to the sacraments, who loves our Lady and the saints; yet, who at the same time has a very poor personal prayer life. Many, even after years of living the life of a good Catholic, have never gone beyond the stages of attending Mass and saying the Rosary. As a result, many of these good Catholics constantly find things "wrong" with the teachings of God and our Church. They will not believe what they don't want to believe. They will cast aside what they feel they don't need or want and tell God that they still love Him and want to go to Heaven. Also, they will be unwilling to accept crosses and they blame God for all the wrong things in their lives.

Because of the lack of spiritual advancement, when a given situation calls for a heroic act of virtue, they are totally unable to perform such an act. For example: they could never practice heroic hope wherein a person finds great inner peace, joy and happiness, in spite of the darkness and pain of daily crosses, just knowing that God loves them and they will share His Heaven of joy for all eternity with Him. They could never practice heroic love for God wherein a person develops a true horror for sin no matter how small and does all in his power to correct his faults and weaknesses solely for the love of God. Most people don't even consider it a sin, but it is, to cheat a little or lie a little or steal a little.

People who lack spiritual advancement could never practice the heroic virtue of love of neighbor wherein the person really cares about the material and spiritual welfare of his neighbor and is willing to spend time helping them–even if this person had at one time hurt or insulted them. Most people are too quick to see their neighbor's faults and sins instead of their needs.

People who are not able to practice heroic virtues could never use the virtue of fortitude to a heroic degree. They could not bear harsh treatment or personal sorrows caused by others in silence with only God as the Witness. They would, instead, seek to get even in one way or another and to loudly complain.

As can be seen by the above examples, practicing heroic virtue not only is out of the ordinary, but also must have very special graces from God.

Before I continue, please allow me to point out the fact that if what you have read shatters your concept of what you thought your own spiritual life was, then do not despair. It is better to know the inaccuracies and mistakes which lie hidden within your union with God than to go on filled with a false security that all is well and "perfect" with your relationship with God. Most lay people, even those involved with all the so-called gifts of the Holy Spirit, have a great deal to learn about true union with God which comes from a well-formed prayer life. If you have found out that you are not as far advanced in union with God or in your prayer life as you thought you were, then that is a good thing to know. Now you can begin to correct the mistakes you have been making so that you can indeed rise to the heights of the prayer of Holy Abandonment with the help of your spiritual director.

Also, and I make a special notation of the following fact: it is not practicing heroic acts of virtue to get all involved with religious activities such as bringing pilgrim statues around from Church to Church, organizing bus trips to shrines or arranging such things as Rosary rallies. While such work for God is excellent and should be encouraged, while it takes a great deal of time and energy, while it brings honor to Mary or to a saint, getting so involved does not mean that the person is doing anything heroic. What the person is doing is using his or her time and energy to work for God and the Church in a special way. But that is only one form of holy charity which we, as Catholics, should constantly perform. I know many people who are doing excellent work giving of themselves and their time to fight abortion. However, such work is not elevated into the area of heroic acts of virtue simply because we should all do what we can to help a good cause if that is possible. Many Catholics waste hours a day or in the evening just having useless conversations or watching T.V. Such wasted time and actions have no merit in the eyes of God. It would be far better for such people to find a few hours a week to help a needy cause. This type of unselfish activity can indeed gain much merit for the person. However, it would never raise the person into the heights wherein heroic acts of virtue can be performed. What is the difference between doing a good deed, even a very difficult good deed, and entering into heroic acts of virtue? The difference is, that many people who have a very poor spiritual life, or a poor prayer life, or have lost sanctifying grace, can do the very same type of activities which people on a high level of union with God can do. They can arrange bus trips or retreats or Rosary rallies even if their souls are not in the state of grace. Often the best worker or organizer who seems to be consumed with love for our Lord or our Lady will leave the Church and grace for one reason or another.

However, when a person has reached the spiritual union of God wherein he or she is capable of performing *heroic acts* of charity, that person has the grace to remain faithful to Christ and His Church at all times.

Please do not misunderstand me. I am not saying that everyone who arranges such an event as a Rosary rally or bus trip to a shrine is in the state of mortal sin or on the way out of the Church. That is not true. What I am saying is that a person in the state of mortal sin or who is about ready to leave the Church can be just as an efficient organizer as a saintly person. That being the case, you can see that even though such a person seems to be doing so much for God and the Church, that person is not practicing heroic acts of virtues by means of organizing rallies or bus trips. The work itself does not make the act heroic or the person a saint.

I have seen many an overeager, busybee worker fall by the wayside when faced with a serious problem. A man I personally know worked harder for our Lady and the Church than anyone I had ever known. He was completely involved in arranging retreats, rallies and bus trips to famous shrines. Yet, in spite of so much religious activity, one day he walked out of our Church into an invalid marriage and became a fallen-away Catholic. All the while he worked so hard for God and for our Lady, his personal prayer life had been a shambles in spite of all his outward religious activities.

Another person I knew was just as energetic a worker for our Lady and our Church. He spent more time than he should have traveling around on all his self-appointed "missions." Suddenly, he was stricken with deadly cancer and he spent his remaining days on earth telling God that He had no right to take his life when he still had so much work to do for the Church. He refused to accept God's holy will and he died a broken, bitter, confused man. I also know the case of a very determined man who destroyed his family life and his marriage because he became obsessed with a religious project of building a special shrine to our Lord. While he worked so hard for the Lord, his poor wife sat home every evening waiting for his return. After the shrine was built, he spent more time there than in his own home. Such work for the Lord was hardly deserving of any merit; and could not be called heroic.

I am also familiar with the following example of why I say that certain types of outward religious activities are not entering into the area of performing heroic acts of virtue. There was a priest whom everyone thought of as being a living saint. His pet project was taking a statue of our Lady into people's homes and organizing groups of women who would come to these homes to say the Rosary. There was a great deal of talk about this priest, stating that he also had the gift of healing, so it was fairly easy for him to get the Rosary groups together. When the women came to say the Rosary or to be "healed," they would all but worship this priest and they treated him as if he were a living saint. The priest found such treatment very much to his liking. He even allowed things which he owned to be given out as precious relics. Then he suddenly died. Shortly after he died, he appeared to a certain woman, from the depths of purgatory suffering most intensely.

The woman was amazed at the condition of the priest whom everyone had declared to be a great saint. She asked: "But what about all the Rosaries you had said? What about all the love you got for our Lady from so many people? Does that not count now in your favor?"

The priest sadly answered: "No, because I caused the people to love me and not our Lady!"

I am, by no means, belittling honest efforts by those who want to get involved in such activities as organizing rallies, bus trips, retreats, etc. Many people who do have a close union with God love to do such things. However, as I said, these activities do not constitute heroic acts of virtue. They are excellent ways and means to bring honor and glory to God or to our Lady, but such activities *do not* make the person a saint. Heroic acts of virtue *do* make a person a saint. Far too often there is human pride or an emotional release contained in outward activities; and as I said, even a person whose soul is in the state of mortal sin can engage in such projects.

However, once a person has reached the heights of the wondrous prayer of Holy Abandonment, wherein heroic acts become part of the person's life, there is never one ounce of pride or emotions involved. Performing heroic acts of virtue requires a great deal of very special grace given solely by God to the person. God does not give such grace to just anyone. A person must prepare his or her soul to receive these special gifts and God never gives such gifts to sinners or to people filled with pride and self-glory.

Now, how would a person know if he or she has or has not actually reached the prayer of Holy Abandonment? Most spiritual writers, including myself, would merely say: "You will know, no one has to tell you!" Or to put it another way, once when I asked my confessor a certain question about a state of union with God, he quickly replied: "If you were there, you would not have asked that question, you would have known the answer."

However, such an explanation is not very helpful for one who sincerely desires the heights of union with God, so I will explain more. But before I do, one word of caution. Remember that what you will read is one of the highest forms of union with God.

Please do not read the words as though it is the state of union which "everyone" is supposed to have. If you read the words believing that you should be this far advanced in your quest for holiness, you could very well destroy the union which you do possess by thinking that what I describe is not your daily prayer life. If you read these words and decide that you are far below this state of union with God, you might become very discouraged and give up your search for holiness. Yet, in reality, you might already have a beautiful solid union with God, but on a lower level.

Now, what is the best way for you to know if you have or have not reached the heights of prayer called Holy Abandonment? First of all, you will be able to see what effects such a union with God has within your daily life; because, such a high state of prayer will show within every aspect of your daily life. There will be no mistaking the positive results of living a life in total union with God's holy will. You will know, without any doubts, that God has called you into this way of life.

However, before these last stages can be reached, the person must already be living a life of virtue, goodness, love for God and neighbor and obedience to the ways and teachings of God and of our Church. The person must have a solid foundation, to build upon, of a pure humility and desire to grow in grace and holiness and must have a deep love for the sacraments. In addition, sin (even small venial sins) must be held in check. As one person explained to me: "I look out there, outside of my life, and see sin, small sins as well as mortal sins, then I raise my hand and say, "Do not come near me, stay where you are!" That high level of sanctity sounds as if it could be the "top" of THE LADDER OF PERFECTION, but it is not. As holy as such a state or degree of union with God is, it still is not Holy Abandonment. Why?

That is a very important question because if a person does indeed possess the holiness I have just described, it would seem that the person is a saint able to perform heroic acts of virtue. But that may not be true because as high a degree of union with God as such a state seems to be, the person could still be plagued with doubts and fears about God's love for him or her or about his or her love for God. The person could still doubt the abilities to receive and use grace. The person could still doubt God's mercy and have guilt feelings about past sins. In addition, the person could still be unable to accept crosses. I am never surprised when a person, whom I had thought had reached a certain state of holiness, confesses to me that he or she still has a great deal of fears and doubts about God or His love for the person or who cannot carry crosses.

The reason why the doubts and fears are still there is that the person's soul has not as yet been purified to the degree desired by God. As a result, not only is the soul still in the state of purification but the person could easily fall from even a high state of union with God. How would such a thing be possible? Simply because the person has not as yet tasted the wondrous, sweet fruits of Holy Abandonment, which can only be obtained after a very long purging of the soul.

It is this need for purging of the soul which is often neglected in lessons about acquiring holiness. The writings may mention accepting crosses and overcoming sins but the true purging involves much, much more if the person allows God to so purge the soul. If allowed, God helps to purify the soul by sending it waves of darkness and spiritual dryness as well as an endless number of spiritual setbacks.

It is interesting to note that many people who have a dramatic encounter with Christ or the Holy Spirit (such as people who claimed they are reborn or baptized anew) soon find that they still have many faults and weaknesses. They had thought they were completely changed. Perhaps they did give up a life of sin, which is to their credit; however, they still walk in a great deal of darkness as far as living an active spiritual life goes. I once read a book by a woman who claimed to have been baptized anew, whose spiritual life was still filled with much darkness, fear and doubt. Throughout her book she gave example after example of "reborn" women who could not understand or respect their own husband's lack of interest in their "new" way of life. These women's reactions were typical human ones. While they may have had an encounter with Christ or the Holy Spirit, this encounter did not automatically purify their souls. They still had a long way to go to reach any type of a lasting union with God. They still had much to learn and much to understand. They still had to pass through many and varied types of purifications.

It is this purification of the soul which is of prime importance if a person is to reach the final stage of union with God and, as I said, this can only take place after a long period (often years) of sufferings, sacrifices, falls and rises, etc.

In addition, there has to be (without any exceptions) the gradual rise of the person's prayer life from vocal prayers into the areas of meditation and then into stages of contemplation. That alone could take years to accomplish.

In the day and age of instant "everything," holiness was added to that list. As a result, a person was taught that the instant "born again" type of holiness was all a person needed to live the life of a saint. Many non-Catholic religions and Bible groups began to spring up "instant" ways to salvation and holiness. They taught that all a person needed for salvation and holiness was a statement saying that he or she believed Christ was the Savior and Lord. Even some misinformed Catholics began to believe in this instant sort of holiness which could be had without the need for a life of mortification, prayer or the sacraments. They cast aside the need for purification and the gradual elevation of one's prayer life by degrees. Fortunately, the spiritual books of the great saints are still available so such mistakes can be corrected.

As I said, the reason why some people in high level of union with God can still fall away into mortal sin or go back into a lower level is that they have not as yet tasted the wondrous, sweet fruits of Holy Abandonment. That is a very important difference between the level of true Holy Abandonment and a lesser union with God. Once these fruits are tasted, once the magnificent lights, peace and joys of Holy Abandonment are within the person's spiritual life, there is no way the person will fall from these lofty heights. He or she is too close to perfect, complete union with God in Heaven to ever wish for anything which could lead to serious sin or away from union with God.

Chapter 3

HOW TO PREPARE FOR THE PRAYER
OF HOLY ABANDONMENT

Now, before you can be drawn by God up to the heights of the mountain where grows the magnificent fruits of Holy Abandonment, it is not only important to have the correct knowledge and motivation but, in addition, there has to be a very special preparation made to enter upon this journey.

The word preparation might cause a bit of discouragement at first because, after all, the whole climb up the ladder begins with one preparation after another. Why then, when the top of the ladder comes into view, is it necessary to make still another type of preparation? However, these new attempts to make the soul ready for final union with God, as final as can be obtained on earth, (the total complete union can only come after death in Heaven) are of upmost necessity inasmuch as they consist of an entire series of spiritual exercises unlike what has already been experienced. During the lower stages of prayer, the emphasis has been upon conquering sins, fault, weaknesses and upon reaching out to the Heart of God through prayer which is often forced or filled with dryness. In addition, the person must have a great deal of determination to rise again when a fall from grace occurs. All such activities take a great deal of effort and require a great deal of daily even hourly attention. There can hardly be one more activity or preparation squeezed into a busy life.

However, the new type of preparation, so that a person may enter into the state of Holy Abandonment (if it is God's will), can become part of a daily life no matter how busy that life is. Not

only that, but the person will desire, with his or her whole heart
and soul, to make an attempt to prepare the soul in such a way.

Now, the first thing to remember about the final stages of Holy
Abandonment is that the actual stage or state of this noble prayer
life is one of queenly delicacy and refinement. That being the
case, it must be handled with utmost care and tenderness. It is as
if a person must "tip toe" into this stage (as a mother "tip toes" to
see her sleeping child) so as not to disturb one small particle of
its precious treasures or exquisite beauty. The person knows it is
dealing with a very, very special and priceless object and wants
to do all things, in acquiring it, so as not to break even a tiny point
of its elegant design.

Within the stages or degrees of prayer life a person can experience many explosive moments such as: wild temptations, strong
loss of faith, many falls and rises, people questioning God's holy
will, numerous complaints, many periods of seeing no reasons to
continue the prayer program, many falls into sins (even mortal
sins), much self-analyzing and agony, and so forth. Such types of
spiritual problems *do not* present themselves within the final
stages of the prayer of Holy Abandonment. I say *stages* because,
do not forget that as with all the different forms of the prayer life
within each one there are many different degrees of that same
stage. For example, one person may be in the beginning of mental
prayer but to a lower degree than someone else. One simply
cannot say there are, for example, four different stages within
a complete prayer life: 1. Vocal prayer, 2. Meditation, 3.
Contemplation, 4. Holy Abandonment. One has to say that it
might take years to perfect each type of prayer so as to advance
into the next stage. During this type of preparation, the person
may pass through several different degrees of that particular type
of prayer life.

Once a person decides to prepare himself or herself to enter
into the stages of Holy Abandonment, the person cannot suddenly burst through the barrier and say: "Here I am! I made it!"
There has to be a preparation which is far more intense than any
made before during the lesser stages of the prayer life. The person must pass through several different degrees of preparation

before the final call from God can be heard deep within the soul, which will enable it to finally enter the brilliant "interior castle" as Saint Teresa of Avila called it. I can compare this preparation to a baby crawling along, inch by inch, towards the goal of standing, walking and finally running.

A person has to learn all the A B C's and 1,2,3's of each phase of the prayer life; however, with this final stage or state of Holy Abandonment in addition the person must learn how to sing songs which he or she has never heard before. Only after he or she has mastered them, only then, can the person taste the sweet fruits of Holy Abandonment.

All that which I have just explained sounds as if the state of Holy Abandonment is most elusive and perhaps unattainable. That is partly true. This stage of prayer life is so far advanced that it actually rests upon the edge of Heaven. It can be safely said that when a person reaches such a state, he or she lives more in Heaven than on earth and he or she sees things more through the eyes of God than through his or her own eyes and thinks more as God would rather than as humans would. However, the person does not think, see or act as would a fanatic. The difference between the two is obvious. The fanatic is not at all interested in what God sees, does or thinks, but only in what he or she does thinks or sees.

Also, you must know that the state of Holy Abandonment can be deceptive at times. A person may think that he has at *last* reached the stage of prayer life only to discover that what he thought sure was Holy Abandonment was something far less. Fortunately, the false union quickly reveals itself by way of the person's falls into periods of discouragement, depression or dryness, etc.; all of which constantly show up in lesser prayer stages but *are not* present in the final stage of Holy Abandonment.

When reached, seldom if ever does a person fall into periods of discouragement or lose the wondrous peace, joy and happiness which these final stages bring. If perchance the joys start to slip away, a correction in the situation will be made immediately. If a fault makes an unwanted appearance, a penance is quickly sought and done. Why? Because the person wants no such disturbances which can distort, in the slightest, the wondrous love song between the soul and its object of affection. Such an analysis upon the part of the person, which enables him or her to quickly detect an out-of-tune note within the rapturous melody of Holy Abandonment, is not only incredible but becomes, in itself, one of the fruits of this union and a most unique virtue.

So, with all such facts taken into consideration, it can be seen why a person has to make a very special preparation in order to enter into this type of a prayer life or union with God.

As I have already said, in this chapter, this preparation will be totally unlike any other type found in the lesser prayer forms. For one reason, if one *has actually* advanced to the threshold of the prayer of Holy Abandonment, the person must, of necessity, *have already* passed through the lower forms of purifications and preparations. The person must be already living a very holy, saintly life and have a very deep, pure love for God and virtue. So there is no need to repeat the same type of a preparation or even the same degree of purification which one went through while entering into lesser prayer stages. If such preparations and purifications had not already been made, the person simply would be in no condition to advance into the prayer of Holy Abandonment.

So, the preparation to try and reach the final state of union with God can begin only after all other degrees of union have been reached or obtained. It is foolish to assume that a person can jump into the highest form of prayer life without passing through the lowest or lesser forms (the lowest being simple, plain vocal prayers such as to merely pray during Mass or to say the Rosary). That is why an instant conversion or burst of joy when Christ is "found" is not the end but only the beginning of a prayer life.

Now, exactly what does this new and different type of preparation consist of? Well, the first very important difference is that the soul no longer wants to become *closer* to God, for it has found its *closeness*. Now it wants to learn what this closeness means. In other words, the soul has found the Sacred Heart of God, the soul has felt the love from the Heart of God, now the soul longs to learn the secrets of that love and of the Heart of God.

It is for that reason why the final stages of Holy Abandonment become so delicate and elusive. It is for that reason why it is God alone who can call the soul into that wondrous state of union with Him. God, as a rule, does not reveal the deep secrets of His love and of His Heart to just anyone. Only in rare cases will God become so intimate with a soul.

The secrets of love within the Heart of God are so overpowering, so awesome, so consuming that the average person would become utterly crushed beneath their intensity if such treasures were revealed to him suddenly without any preparation.

Even a soul which has reached great holiness by and through the other stages of the prayer life would become bewildered and confused by the sheer magnitude of what lies deep within the Heart of God if a soul were not properly prepared to share such.

What are these secrets? They are what I call the fruits of the union with God called Holy Abandonment.

The secrets which I am mainly referring to are contained in Christ's words: "whosoever sees me sees the Father" (*John* 14:9). And in these words: "Be perfect as my Father in Heaven is perfect" (*Matthew* 5:48). What secrets lie hidden within the Heart of love of Christ which prompted such utterances? What mysteries made Christ, in His human nature, one with God, His Father? But more? What secrets lie deep within the very being of God which makes it possible for us human beings, created creatures, to become exposed to and to share the very same perfection which is shared between the Father and the Son? And when shared, what unimaginable treasures can be discovered therein?

If we can reach such a perfection which will enable us to cry out as did Saint Paul: "It is not I, but Christ who lives in me" (*Galatians* 2:20), what portion will God permit us to share and understand of His own divine nature?

Ah, that is what the soul longs to discover when it has advanced to the stages beyond the lower levels found in the prayer life.

And that knowledge or sharing on Christ's part of His most precious secrets is what is so elusive within the limited areas of the prayer life of Holy Abandonment.

Only the most careful preparation can permit Christ to open the guarded doors of His hidden life and allow the chosen soul to enter. In that case, it is the *preparation* of the soul which should become the goal to reach and not so much the entering into the final stage of the union with God called Holy Abandonment.

Does that mean that the person must withdraw himself completely from the world so that he can live a life of total contemplation and aloneness as a preparation for this final state? How else can one prepare for such an awesome state of union with God? It appears, from what I have described, that it would take a whole lifetime of silent contemplation just to get some ideas as to what the state of Holy Abandonment really means, let alone attempt to prepare one's soul to enter such a union with God. How could a person ever hope to do such a thing? Well, the ideal situation would be to run away from the world into a place of silence and prayer as did many saints. However, I am writing this book for people who have duties and obligations which they must attend to and which keep them going from morning until night. What can they do to prepare themselves for the possibility of entering into the highest stage of union with God?

First of all, remember that God *alone calls the soul into this final state;* so do not even think about sharing all those secrets with God through your own efforts. Concentrate instead upon learning the ways of the preparation and not upon the final results. This will make you feel more confidence in yourself and more able to cope with the task before you. Also, realize that you must not underestimate the value of the preparation itself. While the final results bring about the supreme union with God, complete with all its merits, graces and spiritual treasures, each step taken by way of preparation has within itself its own wondrous spiritual treasures which can become yours and last for all eternity.

To begin the preparation which leads to the call from Christ into the center of the prayer of Holy Abandonment, your whole spiritual program has a new and different starting point which actually is the end of the lesser spiritual programs.

In the earlier programs (or preparations) for the lesser forms of prayer life, the central point was self-improvement. The goal to reach was overcoming sins, faults, weaknesses and acquiring virtues. You had to reach out and attempt to touch Christ who waited and watched as you struggled towards Him on unsteady feet. He was somewhere in front of you and became the reason why you were so willing to overcome sins and acquire virtues. You saw Him waiting. You longed for Him and His love. And if you found obstructions which prevented your union with Him, your soul languished in agony until they were overcome.

Also, as you struggled to conquer barriers which were constantly being placed before you, you barely had time to breathe as you struggled up that ladder through different prayer stages because you had so much to do just to keep inching along towards your goal.

However, in the advance stage of preparation for the final union with God, the agony disappears and is replaced by a song of victory. Yet this song is not exuberant. It is sung as if you are only learning the notes and melody. It will require much practice to master the magnificent notes and words for it is most intricate and is a song which you never heard before. Still it thrills you and brings immense joy. You will know that as soon as you are able to hear the distant sound of this melody that you have entered upon a level of spiritual advancement which contains far more sunshine and peace than darkness and battles. Not only that, but the *closeness* to Christ, from whom the sunshine emerges, is breathless. He now appears a very real, clearly seen person and not merely as a shadow in the far distance whom you desperately wanted to reach and to know. Not only is this person of Christ nearer to you than you could ever have imagined but He becomes a "different" Christ than you ever could imagine existed. For now He reveals a slight bit (only a tiny portion) of Himself as the second person of the Blessed Trinity. You begin to see Him, not so much as the human Christ, the person who died upon that cross as your Savior but you begin to see and to know Him as the Infinite God who created the heavens, the universe and the earth and you.

It is then—and only then—when you begin to see Christ as the total center of all, especially your own daily existence and you want to enter into His secrets.

Remember that in order to reach such a state of union with God you must have, of necessity, acquired tremendous grace and virtue as you climbed to the summit of THE LADDER OF PER-FECTION. This grace and virtue is what is needed to see and understand God in His role as the Infinite, Almighty Creator. Without the grace and all the preparations and purifications, you would neither recognize nor understand the God who stands upon the top rung of the ladder.

Now, the preparation to enter into a closer, more intimate union with God becomes, almost overwhelming in the desires to do just that. Yet, always you must remember that not one single over-whelming desire is in anyway fanatical nor false. At this point of spiritual development, the soul is completely in tune with God's holy will. And by the way, this "being in tune" is a free act of the will. This is what the soul desperately wants. The person could still choose to stop all advancement, to give up completely or even to fall away into sin. Yet, that is almost impossible due to the soul's tremendous desires to enter deeper into the love and secrets of the very Heart of God. This situation can be compared to a young woman who longs to be united with her beloved one in holy matrimony and he to her. For no reason is she going to refuse the beautiful engagement diamond when it is offered to her. She has already chosen, with her own free will, to take the step into marriage. That is why the spiritual state which I am now speaking about is often referred to as the "spiritual or mystical marriage." The soul is not going to refuse this final union with the Beloved One.

At this point, the soul still *has not* entered into the state of Holy Abandonment, but has only been filled with grace and the desires to prepare his or her soul for this spiritual state. As I said, only God can call the soul into the center of the prayer of Holy Abandonment.

Also, this preparation is not going to be delayed. The soul plunges itself into this preparation as if it had found a pool of refreshing water in the desert.

The first thing the person does is to place Christ as the center of all his or her thoughts, words, desires and actions. It is from

Christ, in the center, where the whole spiritual program of this preparation emerges. Now you no longer want to "find" Christ, or to be "near" Him but to, at all times, please Him and bring Him joy. Note the difference between this preparation and the ones in the lower prayer stages. In the lower stages, the soul longs to have Christ *bring him joy.* In this higher state, the soul's one desire is to bring Christ joy and to please Him, no matter at what cost to the soul. It then becomes a joy, for example, to suffer for Christ. That is why great saints did severe penances with much joy; even though, they committed few if any sins.

Also, note another important difference between the lower stages of prayer and this advanced stage. In the lower stages there are the separate prayer forms called: vocal, meditation and contemplation. These prayers require a person to set aside a certain time for prayer. In most cases, the person sets aside a time to go to Mass, to say the Rosary, to meditate or to enter into the prayer of deep contemplation. After such periods of prayer, God is often forgotten as the material life takes over the person's words, deeds and thoughts. That is why it is still possible for a person, even a holy, virtuous person, to fall into sin and to give in to human weaknesses. In addition, the person can still become very depressed, sad, discouraged and refuse to accept God's will in a given matter.

Many people I know, whom I would consider to be religious, holy, good people, can become deeply depressed if illness suddenly strikes someone they love or themselves.

Such a thing would not happen when a person advances into the higher preparation for a call into the prayer life of abandonment, the person not only prays, but actually makes the prayer of Holy Abandonment a way of life. This prayer then is not only vocal prayer or meditation at a given time of the day but the prayer found in the preparation and also in Holy Abandonment becomes a *way of life* which is lived daily and even hourly!

There is no need to set aside a special hour to pray, because the person's soul is at all times in a state of prayer, even among worldly duties and distractions. Of course, there will be time set aside for special prayers and for Mass. Because one of the joys reserved for this high spiritual state is a tremendous joy found in prayer and during the Mass. However, when the prayer time ends, when the Mass is over, when the meditation periods conclude, the soul remains in a very deep state of interior prayer and joy which does not leave it, even if the person continues to live a very, very busy demanding type of life filled with a "million" distractions.

This ability to have the soul remain in a very deep state of interior prayer among material conditions simply does not happen in the lower spiritual stages of union with God. For example, just try to say only one "Our Father" while working in a busy office or factory. See how far you have gotten by the end of the day. Chances are you never even finished the one "Our Father" during the whole eight-hour workday. But in the final stages of preparations, of which I am talking about, the soul had developed such a repertoire of love-filled prayers and praises to give to Christ, who is the total center of the soul's existence, that these prayers spring almost automatically from the depths of the soul's inner being without interruptions.

In the same office type of work-situation which I have described, the soul can still send prayers of love and praise to Christ in spite of the noises of such a location. The soul can immediately withdraw into itself, where dwells the Almighty God and hold onto His hand in a very deep, mystical sort of way after each material duty is attended to.

By the time the soul has reached these advanced spiritual stages of preparation and after God calls it into Holy Abandonment, the soul is so fused to God and to His holy will that ordinary distractions cannot separate the two. Nor can such distractions prevent the soul from singing its love song to God and hearing His love song return in all its sweetness.

In the lower forms of spirituality, the distractions which occur in the person's daily life, and even show up during prayer time, cause the person much anguish and torment. But when the soul enters into the higher union with God, this anguish and torment disappear because the soul and God are so together as one and the love song continues without interruptions in such a way that the person, who may be in the middle of a distraction, can merely in one second raise his whole being to God and feel the sweetness of the love shared between them. Needless to say, this is a most wondrous, beautiful state to be in and when reached, one can say that all the sufferings, agony and anguish of the lower stages of union with God were as "nothing" compared to the sweetness of the love song which the soul now shares with its beloved, divine Guest.

The sweet notes of this love song came from the person being in tune with the melody it hears deep within its being. This song is a two-part harmony, one part sung by Christ and the other by the soul.

However, when the soul is only in a state of preparing for Holy Abandonment and has not as yet been called into that prayer life, there can occur many notes of the love song which are out-of-tune. The soul as yet has not learned the melody and must sort out its own mistakes. Also, the song itself is very faint at first and very delicate. It is, at this point, the beginning of the preparation, so distant and fragile that the soul must be on constant alert not to allow it to merely drift away or to become distorted. The whole preparation for Holy Abandonment becomes, then, the soul's task to learn the correct notes and melody so as to be in perfect tune with Christ.

All that means is that the soul must be in tune with God's holy will. Christ and the soul must be one in desires, thoughts and deeds. All that the person does, thinks, desires and acts must be done in complete harmony with Christ's holy will. The soul must condition itself to be able to hear, in an instant, one note which may be made harsh or out of tune by its own desires or actions, so that these thoughts, desires or actions can be corrected as soon as possible. The soul longs to hear, at all times, the sweet melody in all its purity and clarity. Only then can it learn more of the secrets which are contained deep within this love song. It is only after the soul is able to sing in perfect harmony this love song when it becomes ready for the call from Christ to enter into the state of Holy Abandonment.

This is what is known as living a total Christ-centered way of life or as Saint Paul tells us: "It is not I, but Christ who lives in me" (*Galatians* 2:20). Very, very few people, religious as well as lay people, actually live this Christ-centered way of life. They may be, as I said, holy, pious, religious people filled with a pure love for God; all of which developed after a long time of being faithful to a personal spiritual program centered around the sacraments and prayer. However, they still have not advanced into the higher levels of spirituality wherein Christ is the complete core around which their daily lives revolve.

They still can have spiritual problems which bring forth such a thing as to doubt God's love for them. They can still refuse to accept all crosses and burdens of their daily lives. At times, it may seem to them that the good Lord, His love and ways seem unreal and far, far away from daily realities. In other words, they still are in lower prayer forms and have yet to enter into the higher ones; even though, as I said they are already well-advanced into sanctity and holiness.

As I have explained, when one enters into the preparation for Holy Abandonment, the problems which I just mentioned disappear and the person begins his preparation by beginning to actually live a Christ-centered way of life.

By the time a person is ready to prepare his soul for the final call of Christ into the prayer of Holy Abandonment, all such spiritual battles have to have been fought and won. There can be no doubts about God's love for the person or his own love for God. There can be no doubts about the fact that Christ is indeed the center of one's daily life. He is not only very much alive but very near to the person as well. There has to be these absolute certainties concerning God's love and presence or else there can be no further advancement into a deeper union with God.

Now, how does one actually learn the correct notes of the love song I have just mentioned? How is one able to pick out the out-of-tune notes which distort the melody?

The answer to both questions lies in the type of spiritual life which the person is already living when he decides to prepare a program for greater spiritual union with God. Remember that you prepare your own spiritual programs, God does not. You, with your spiritual director, decide which is the best path for you to follow. God cooperates by sending you the necessary graces to carry out the program; but you decide, with your own free will, what you will try to accomplish.

That being the case, by the time you have reached the final stages for preparation to enter into the prayer of Holy Abandonment, you already have been following a program of self-improvement overcoming sins, faults and weaknesses and acquiring virtues. You have already learned what happens within your soul and spiritual life if you fall and commit a sin. You already know the agony of defeat and the joys of victory.

Now, in this final stage of preparation you become more in tune with God's will for you by polishing the virtue of self-knowledge. You will continue with your spiritual program of overcoming faults and weaknesses and acquiring virtue. However, there will be a vast difference between what happens in this preparation and what happened in the preparations for the lesser prayer stages. Now, you will want to be so much in tune with God's holy will that you will discover, see and understand many faults or lack of virtue which you never realized you had! In lesser stages, your most glaring sins, faults and weaknesses were very obvious; and overcoming them was a task so engrossing that small faults and weaknesses went completely unnoticed.

However, before any soul can enter into the prayer of Holy Abandonment, these unnoticed, tiny faults and weaknesses must be noticed and corrected because they become the out-of-tune notes which distort that beautiful song of love between the soul and Christ. Now you become an artist who puts the finishing touches to his masterpiece.

One day a gifted artist showed his painting to a friend who thought it to be magnificent. Yet the artist replied: "It is still not finished. Come back next week and the painting will be completed."

The friend returned in a week and the painting was now ready to be sold.

"But, the friend said in amazement, "I see no difference! It looks exactly the same as it did last week! It was finished then."

The painter smiled and answered: "No, it was not finished last week. Since then I have put in many fine lines which had not been there. Oh, maybe, you did not know they were missing, but I did!"

In like manner, now the person, who imitates the artist, sees tiny faults within himself or herself which no one else notices, but which he knows causes him or her to be out-of-tune in a life which is Christ-centered.

How could such a thing be possible? Again grace steps into the picture. The more you increase grace, the more you will be able to see yourself as God sees you. The more you increase grace, (sanctifying grace) the closer becomes your union with God. As this union draws you more and more into a Christ-centered life of perfection, the more clearly will you see your own imperfections because the more clearly will you see and understand Christ's perfection. As you begin to enter deeper and deeper into the secrets of perfection which dwell in the Heart of God, your desires for your own perfection will increase so that all you do will be a true, clear reflection of the perfection of Christ's. That being the case, your preparation to enter into the final stages of Holy Abandonment will center more and more upon your desires to become a true, clear, in-tune reflection of Christ's own perfection. This, you know, will bring great joy to God's Heart and to your own and He may, indeed, call you most lovingly into the state where you can, at last, taste the indescribable sweetness of the fruits of the prayer called Holy Abandonment.

Chapter 4

THE BUSY PERSON AND INTERIOR MORTIFICATION

Now comes the problem: how can a person arrive at and enter into such a sublime preparation when he or she is constantly living with the stress and pressures found in a normal life?

If the person has indeed acquired a great deal of holiness and desires to enter into the preparation for a call from Christ into the final stages of Holy Abandonment what must he or she do, especially if he or she is a very, very busy person in a very noisy, everyday sort of life?

The secret is called interior mortification. I have mentioned this virtue before. But to mention it is one thing to explain what it means is another; however, to actually live the life of interior mortification is quite another thing altogether. Yet, a person must live a life of interior mortification if he or she wants to enter the stage or state of preparation for a call into the highest union with God.

What exactly do I mean by living a life of interior mortification: which must become a part of every spiritual life? By the time you have passed through several prayer stages, you should be familiar with mortification and how it is used to struggle against sins, faults and human weaknesses. A person must mortify or control one's self-will, self-love and passions if he or she is to attempt to live a holy life following God's holy will.

If you have reached these final stages of preparation for Holy Abandonment, you should also be familiar with interior mortification.

Interior mortification is the virtue which enables a person to control thoughts to such a degree that he or she can quickly change material thoughts into spiritual ones. For example, if your mind starts to think about a useless, nonsensical T.V. program or movie, such thoughts become wasted for they produce no merits or eternal rewards. Also, they do steal time away from God. If you practice the virtue of interior mortification, you can quickly change such thoughts into worthwhile, meritorious ones by thinking about God and His infinite love for you. Such thoughts then become the prayer of meditation. Remember that you can dwell upon only one subject at a time within the depths of your thoughts. That is why there are so many annoying distractions during prayers, especially vocal prayers such as the Mass and the Rosary. If, for example, during Mass, your mind starts to wander and you find yourself thinking about golf or dinner or the children, you cannot at the same time think about God and what you are trying to say to Him by means of prayer.

The trick or secret is to change the object or subject that you want to think about. With the virtue of interior mortification, it is possible to catch your mind wandering away from God and prayer and to bring it back to where it belongs.

By the time you are ready to enter into the stages of preparation for Holy Abandonment, you should already be able to quickly change your thoughts from material ones to spiritual ones during times of prayer and in that way destroy many annoying distractions.

But now a greater challenge awaits you. Now, the virtue of interior mortification must be perfected in such a way that it can be used in all phases of your daily life as well as when you go to Mass or pray. Now, the virtue of interior mortification also means that as you carry out your daily duties and responsibilities, you must be able to separate in your mind *necessary* thoughts from *useless* distractions and *useless* thoughts. This means that you must take great care to make sure that such useless thoughts and annoyances do not take up the time, in your mind, which should be used to praise and love God.

Allow me to present an example of what I mean. Say that

someone, who is a good friend of yours, suddenly insults you and your feelings are hurt. It is not a sin or even a fault if you dwell upon these nasty remarks and feel a little pain because of them. For in this case you have left behind, as you advanced in the spiritual life, the sins connected with such a situation. You neither want to get revenge nor to hate the person, or other purely human reactions. But you do dwell upon the remarks, in your mind, and suffer because of them. Sometimes this suffering goes on for days and becomes "all" that you think about.

When you attempt to prepare your soul for Holy Abandonment, such thoughts become useless and out-of-tune with the sweet love song you want to sing to your Lord who dwells within your soul. That is where the virtue of interior mortification comes into the picture. When you find yourself thinking such useless thoughts, you use this virtue to change your thoughts from ones of self-pity into ones of love for God's holy will or love for His holy cross. You also can pray for this person instead of thinking about the insults.

If a person is to live a holy life in union with God, to the highest degree or level, that person must be able to change his or her thoughts from material to spiritual ones at all times.

Remember that thought-time, the time spent thinking as you go through each day, is as important to your spiritual life as is prayer-time. It becomes especially important when you are so busy that you cannot spend all the time you want to in actual prayer. Your thoughts become a marvelous opportunity to live a life of prayer and closeness to God, even in a very busy material life; and must be taken into consideration if you want to enter into the higher forms of prayer.

If you honestly analyze many of your thoughts, you will discover that half of them are absolutely useless and a waste of precious thought-time. With the virtue of interior mortification, you will be able to use that precious time to think spiritual thoughts and to pray.

That does not mean that you can no longer think about daily duties, work, studies, getting dinner ready, recreation, etc. Such thoughts are *necessary*. You must pay attention to such things as school work if you are a student, household duties if you have a family to take care of or what the boss tells you if you are being paid to do a certain job.

However, there are many moments during each day when you can change your thoughts from material to spiritual if it is only to tell God that you love Him and will accept all that He wishes to send you. There are also many times during the day when your thoughts are very much self-centered. Most sins are committed because people are so in love with their own ideas, desires and ways. Arguments are started, lies are told, things are stolen, etc. just because a person *thinks* (in his mind) that he or she is justified in committing such acts or deeds. All temptations must be mulled over in one's mind before they are accepted or rejected. Sometimes hours, days or even weeks can be spent thinking about doing something wrong because of pride and self-love. All these human weaknesses, faults and sins can disappear when interior mortification is used to change material thoughts into spiritual ones *as soon as* the temptations begin. If for example, a person makes you angry an argument could be avoided if you change your thoughts to ones such as: "Dear Lord, I accept this cross as penance for my sins."

Along with the useless thoughts, which destroy the thought-time needed to live a more active spiritual life, there has to be taken into consideration useless conversations during the day. Of course, one must carry on all *necessary* conversations. But often a great deal of time is wasted when useless conversations are engaged in. To speak about, for example, a football game or a neighbor's deeds for long periods of time is a waste of precious time and unthinkable when one wants to live the highest form of the prayer life.

That does not mean that all conversations must be spiritual. It means that *useless* conversations must be eliminated. Then when useless thoughts and conversations are controlled, through the virtue of interior mortification, it can be seen that even a very busy person can live a very active, holy spiritual life and find the time to do just that.

What I have just explained is what was always known in convents and monasteries. Whenever you think of or see pictures about nuns, priest, monks or brothers living segregated from the world, in a contemplative life, you will see them or think about them with heads bowed in silence filled with a special kind of inner reflection. What is presented by their whole way of life is a perfect example of interior mortification. Within such a life, all useless thoughts and conversations are rejected. There is an atmosphere of silence and inner peace as they follow their rules. They are allowed only certain times during each day when they can talk and have recreation. At all other times, they take great care to keep themselves away from material distractions.

Of course, lay people or busy nuns and priests cannot go to such extremes; however, they can understand the way material distractions can lead them into many useless thoughts and conversations. For example, many busy housewives have a radio or T.V. loudly playing all day long. Millions of workers spend most of their working hours daydreaming about getting a better job with more money. Such people consume a great deal of thought-time by allowing themselves to fall into these material distractions. Please note that I am referring to distractions and not to sins. For, by the time a person feels ready, and his or her spiritual director agrees, to enter into the preparation for a call into Holy Abandonment, the person should, of necessity, have already conquered most glaring sins, faults and human weaknesses.

When such a person does plan to prepare his or her soul for the final preparations, the person must pay close attention to all the useless distractions in daily life so as to live a life free of them. Only then can he or she have a prayer life filled with inner peace, silence and reflection.

Now, you can more clearly see the complete climb up THE LADDER OF PERFECTION. It starts with the desires for a closer union with God. Then goes into the areas of overcoming mortal sins, venial sins, faults and human weaknesses; while at the same time using grace to acquire and polish all sorts of virtues. Finally this climb reaches the heights of a more active prayer life when the person learns the value of interior mortification and the role that virtue plays in overcoming useless distractions found in his or her daily material life so that such distractions can be put aside while the soul continues its silent prayer life of love for God. Also note that one of the most important parts of all that I have said concerning grace, acquiring virtues, overcoming faults, sins, etc. and using interior mortification, to change material thoughts into spiritual ones, can be done in the busiest of material lives. A person does not have to leave his or her daily duties and obligations in order to follow a spiritual program which will bring the person into a closer union with God. Such a program can be followed by a housewife, a factory worker, a teacher, an office worker, a busy priest or nun, etc. in whatever circumstances the person fulfills each daily responsibility. Because interior mortification takes place deep in the being of the person, he does not have to leave a material life in order to acquire and use this virtue. The whole idea of living an active spiritual life, close to the Heart of God, is to find within one's own state of life the graces necessary to do just that and to weed out all things which interfere with this spiritual plan.

One of the greatest, most prevalent interferences, which prevents the proper spiritual use of a person's thought-time is daydreaming. In addition to changing material thoughts into spiritual ones and weeding out, in the mind, useless thoughts, there has to be an understanding of how daydreaming can destroy the thought-time necessary for a closer union with God. Daydreams are always about situations which will never become realities or have never happened and concern people or places that are far removed from one's own state of life.

Daydreams have a way of activating the imagination to such an extent that it is impossible to create the atmosphere of inner peace and recollection which are so necessary for a high state of union with God.

When people daydream they are always looking outward, someplace else, for that drastic change in their lives which will make such lives become that elusive "Garden of Eden."

Most daydreams in themselves are not sinful nor wrong especially if a person is already well-advanced in the prayer life. But they do manage to creep into even a well-regulated program of spiritual activity because it is so easy to wish to be in a life free from daily crosses and problems. Most people have many crosses to carry each day and they face problems which they would rather not confront. It is not too difficult for a feeling of discouragement to envelop such a person's thoughts and change these thoughts into daydreams. As a result, for example, a woman who has a valid but unhappy marriage will dream about "someday" "if" her marriage could be annulled she would meet her "prince charming" and "live happily ever after."

Study the following example of the way useless daydreams can greatly interfere with a person's union with God; even though, the actual daydream is not sinful. A person (man or woman) finds much to be desired in daily life. The person will dream about the day when a vast fortune will come to him. He will plan to give a percentage to charity (to ease any feelings of guilt for the amount spent on self-interests), to give money to relatives, friends or to merely make all his own dreams come true. Such thought-time is consumed making all sorts of plans concerning money which does not even exist and probably never will.

What are the disastrous spiritual results of such daydreams even if the dreams themselves are not sinful in any way? (Sinful thoughts would be to desire sinful situations or to think about obtaining money the wrong way, such as through a crime, etc.) The first results of such daydreams (and others like this example) are that the person fails to see all the good things in his or her present life. Also there is the tendency to be unable or unwilling to face daily realities and problems. Then it becomes very easy for him or her to lose faith in God because God does not make such dreams come true by sending money or changing situations.

However, as bad as all these results can become, one of the worst results is that, within such a situation, the person fails to see the wondrous spiritual gifts which could be his or hers or which are already possessed. He or she will also overlook and not use numerous graces which could bring much spiritual joy and happiness. The person will not respond to such graces because of daydreams which take him or her out of the real life into a world of make-believe.

Numerous people do attempt to run away from the realities of daily life, not only through daydreams, but through all sorts of pleasures. There are books to be read, shows to see, T.V. programs to turn on, music to be heard, etc. While there are many pleasures as innocent as daydreams, all these distractions end up within the mind of the person and take away an enormous amount of thought-time which could be used to love God and send Him thoughts of pure love for His will.

When a person wants to advance into high forms of prayer, the person must be able to constantly guard against the waste of precious thought-time. So you can understand how important the virtue of interior mortification is and how it is used to rid one's mind of useless thoughts and distractions.

Note also, that interior mortification is used not only to rid one's mind of useless thoughts and distractions but to turn one's thoughts towards Christ. The beauty of this virtue is seen when one uses it to *turn away* from self and self-interests and to *turn to* Christ and His ways.

The more you rid your mind of useless thoughts, which are centered around self, the more you can center your whole life around Christ, His love and His will for you. When that happens, then your deeds, words and actions become one with Christ. Then, no matter what you do or think or say, (even in a busy life) you act, think and speak as if Christ was there watching you approving all.

To live a life of interior mortification becomes, then, a very important part of a program of complete self-forgetfulness. And such a program can be followed no matter how busy the material life is. That is the way to detach oneself from material things without changing one's state of life. As long as grace can be obtained, and it can be, then a person can make Christ the center of his or her life no matter how busy that life becomes.

In such a Christ-centered life, all virtues can be obtained through grace, can be polished and used daily.

No matter what type of work you do, office, factory, housework, religious, etc., it is possible to increase grace through prayer and the sacraments. With this grace you can live a Christ-centered life of exterior and interior mortification. Then you can continue your daily life but in such a way that you will bring great joy to Christ and also to yourself.

It is this part about bringing great joy to yourself, but especially to Christ, which separates this final preparation to enter the highest form of prayer from the lower stages of the prayer life.

In the lower prayer stages, there is a constant battle between temptations, self-love, self-will, self-interests and grace and virtue. These battles take away much spiritual joy and the soul longs to receive consolations from Christ because it is unable to produce for itself a joy to give to Him or to keep.

In this final preparation, the soul can give joy to Christ and to oneself merely by changing thoughts and desires to ones which are Christ-centered.

Notice that I said to change one's thoughts and desires. I did not say to change one's lifestyle, such as to leave family, friends, jobs, etc. For it is indeed very possible to keep one's thoughts and desires Christ-centered no matter what tasks and duties keep the person occupied. Also, remember what I said that before such a high state of spirituality can be achieved, the person must already have passed through much purification and already be living a holy, virtuous life. But even so, such a holy life may not be as Christ-centered as the type of life I am talking about. The person may not commit actual sins, or be filled with dire weaknesses, but he or she may still have many useless thoughts and desires which must be controlled. It is this control which becomes the final preparation for being called by Christ into the prayer of Holy Abandonment.

Chapter 5

THE WONDROUS FRUITS
OF HOLY ABANDONMENT

The fruits or results of living a life of true abandonment to God's holy will are reserved for the final stages of the prayer of Holy Abandonment. As can be seen by all I have written about the different levels or degrees of prayer, these final stages can be reached only after a long series of spiritual experiences which begin and end with the acquisition of grace. As I have said so often, a person cannot merely "jump" to the top of THE LADDER OF PERFECTION, in one moment, no matter how "close" to God a person feels at that moment. There not only has to be a long series of grace-inspired spiritual experiences but there also has to be a long series of instructions and lessons to learn. It is well to remember that *knowing* what has to be done is equally as necessary as to prepare the way through prayer, grace and the ordinary means of sanctification.

Spiritual instructions and guidance are a must. That is why, within the walls of convents and monasteries, there are lessons given in the correct way to climb THE LADDER OF PERFECTION.

Why are such lessons so important? Or to put it another way: why do you have to learn the way to closer union with God, can He not show you the way all by Himself?

Oh, I am sure that He can do just that through infused knowledge and no doubt He has done such a thing on rare occasions. But such occasions remain just that, very rare and far between. God does not usually "grab" a soul and lift the person to the top of the ladder. Why would He not do such a thing as the rule? Well, for one reason, a sudden revelation of Himself and all the wondrous fruits of total union with Him would only confuse and even frighten a soul which is not *capable* of understanding what is happening. Only grace, and a superabundance of grace, can prepare a soul and bring it into a condition wherein the person can fully understand what the prayer of Holy Abandonment is all about.

Many people, whom I knew, who were very close to God and who were already living a very active spiritual life were unable to understand what the prayer of Holy Abandonment was all about. The very word "Abandonment" actually frightened them. They thought that if they did indeed get involved in such a high form of prayer, they would lose all their freedoms and not be able to function in their daily lives. They "hold back" and did not even want to attempt to climb to such heights. However, with the proper spiritual lessons and direction, such a timid soul can learn the way to the prayer of Holy Abandonment and taste its wondrous and satisfying fruits.

Also, such lessons and direction are of upmost importance because even with grace, a person does *not* always "just naturally" follow paths of holiness and sanctity. A person does not just easily glide along on wings of perfection to a closer union with God. A person does not just automatically place himself or herself within the areas of developing a very deep union with God.

There can be too many mistakes, slips and misses along the road to perfection. Human nature with all its weaknesses is simply not geared for perfection. The truth is that such a way of life is totally against human nature. There is a constant clash between the supernatural way of living with grace and the natural way of the human side of life. The soul is willing to follow God but the body is weak and often puts up a strong resistance.

Everyone knows what happens when someone is not brought up or taught the correct way of living a good, decent, moral lifestyle. The person will just naturally give in to all human weaknesses and become a very selfish, greedy, sinful person. From the simple lessons taught a child by its mother about not telling a lie, to the advance lessons about entering into the prayer of Holy Abandonment, there is always a great need for the proper direction and instructions.

Also, there has to be taken into consideration the fact that God does not interfere with man's free will. God gives man grace and the opportunities to receive sufficient grace to save souls; however, He leaves man on his own when it comes to improving man's relationship with his Creator. That is the main reason why man finds it so easy to sin and fall away from God's ways. God does not tie a rope on man's free will to bind it to His own. When man loves his Creator and gives his mind, heart and soul to this Creator, God wants such giving to be pure and freely offered.

It is the fact that we do have free will which makes it necessary for us to learn about the different steps which have to be taken to climb that ladder to a closer union with God. Each step we take must be a free action or else it cannot profit the person's spiritual life. In order for the person to freely want to climb each step of that ladder, the person has to know what he is doing and be willing to do it. That is where the lessons and knowledge come into the picture.

Even with an instant conversion, such as St. Paul's, still he had to learn what being a Christian was all about and he had to freely follow the lessons he learned. Just to say that you love God with your whole heart and soul and mind does not automatically teach you how to express that love in your daily life. Even with grace, and the inspiration of the Holy Spirit, there still has to be a knowledge of how to use grace and a motivation which enables the person to freely use grace the way God wants it to be used.

Without knowledge and motivation, grace is often lost as can be seen by the examples of fallen-away and lukewarm Catholics. In such cases, it is human nature which becomes the person's guide to life. And human nature filled with human weaknesses just naturally follows paths of sin, self-love, pride and greed.

So, in order to taste the wondrous fruits of the heights of union with God called Holy Abandonment, one must, of necessity, learn and follow a very strict series of rules or instructions about the prayer life. However, while the struggle seems long and extremely difficult, the end results are worth all the sufferings, tears, crosses and pain. The fruits are the most precious possession a person could ever desire and once tasted, they will never be cast aside or ignored.

Now, what are these fruits or rewards after all the struggles to reach the heights of the prayer of Holy Abandonment? When you learn what they are, you will fully understand why all the lessons and instructions are necessary. You will also find the motivations or the reasons why the struggle should continue. For, within these fruits, you will discover total spiritual fulfillment and find what you have been searching for.

FAITH

Up to this point, I have not said too much about faith, because the subject of this book is prayer and how to take the different steps upward to the highest form of prayer called Holy Abandonment. I can only assume that any person who wants a deeper prayer life has a very deep, sincere faith in Christ, the Saviour, His teachings and the teachings of the Catholic Church. But I want to mention faith now because when a person has been called into the prayer of Holy Abandonment, a most beautiful thing happens in regards to a person's faith. The very first fruits of the prayer of Holy Abandonment are the new insights one has concerning faith and the Church's teachings.

As with all virtues, faith can be increased, expanded and polished by grace. Because one major source of grace is prayer (as well as the sacraments) the more one perfects his or her prayer life, the more the person polishes the virtue of faith by and through this grace received.

Faith is a virtue, first infused into a person's soul at Baptism with two other virtues called hope and charity (or love); then brought to completion through the person's love for the faith which has been strengthened and perfected throughout many a battle (or temptations) used by the devil who attempts to destroy that faith.

Why would the devil work so hard to attempt to destroy a person's faith? Because for him to destroy a person's faith is for the devil to gain a soul.

Christ said to His apostles: "Go into the whole world and proclaim the gospel to every creature. Whoever believes and is baptized will be saved; whoever does not believe will be condemned" (*Mark* 16:15-16).

Faith is belief in all that Christ taught and all that Holy Mother Church teaches.

By the time the person reaches the heights of Holy Abandonment (or at least prepared his or her soul for this exalted state of prayer) the person must, of necessity, possess a very strong faith in the teachings of Christ and the teachings and doctrines of Holy Mother Church.

It would make no sense for anyone to attempt to reach a high state of union with God if that person lost faith in his or her Catholic religion. Yet, there are those who attempt to do just that. They claim they love the Lord, and even prayer; yet at the same time, they refuse to go to Mass or receive the sacraments of Confession and the Eucharist. Such a prayer life is a shambles, no matter how loudly they insist that they love God and pray in their "own way," because the very essence or foundation for a solid, meaningful prayer life is missing. That foundation is faith.

During the '70s, '80s and '90s there was a huge ocean of rebellion among the members of society; wherein, people began to "do their own thing." This concept, which became very popular, especially among young people, included religion. As a result, numerous people lost their precious Catholic faith; yet they still insisted that they believed in God and wanted to, some day, find their eternal home in Christ's Heaven of light.

What brought on such rebellion was the lack of two basic virtues needed to protect and preserve faith. These two virtues are humility and obedience.

These two virtues are a necessity if one is to climb THE LADDER OF PERFECTION to a closer union with God. Why? Because a person has to go down into the depths of humility before he or she can rise to the heights of sanctity; and that virtue of humility includes the virtue of obedience.

Obedience to what and to whom? That obedience means to accept and obey all that Christ and His Church teaches. Why the

Church? Because Christ left to His Church the way and the means to obtain the graces necessary for a person's rise to the top of THE LADDER OF PERFECTION through the virtue of faith.

Faith then becomes the key which unlocks the door to holiness and sanctity. Christ said: "And so I say to you, you are Peter, and upon this rock I will build my Church and the gates of hell shall not prevail against it. I will give you the keys to the kingdom of heaven. Whatever you bind on earth shall be bound in heaven; whatever you loose on earth shall be loosed in heaven" (*Matthew* 16:18-19).

Very often, in the lower stages of prayer, the faith needed to advance up that LADDER to a more complete union with God may be far from complete.

A person, whose prayer life is on the lowest level of vocal prayer may go to Mass and say the Rosary; but at the same time, may refuse to accept or believe a teaching of the Church. Such a faith has many flaws in it; and will prevent a higher union with God. Why? Because there remains in the person the human pride which destroys the virtue of humility that is needed to advance into a higher stage of the prayer life.

A person displays that destructive pride when he or she decides to disobey the Church's teachings or to refuse to believe a doctrine of the Church, such as Purgatory.

However, when a person enters into, or prepares to enter into the prayer of Holy Abandonment there are no conflicts regarding faith. If there had been problems in the past, such problems have been solved and done away with. Why do I say that?

Because, the person has used grace to overcome all sins and temptations against faith. There remains only a beautiful inner feeling that the person experiences as he or she acknowledges the fact that the Church, her teachings and doctrines lead the way to personal sanctification and to salvation as well. The person has developed such a strong love for God's holy will, that he or she would never stray from the paths which the Church has created for spiritual growth based upon a pure, a holy faith.

That feeling is not only beautiful to experience, but it gives the person a wondrous freedom; for, to attempt to tell the Church that she is wrong puts chains around the person's faith. Then the person has to constantly look for all sorts of human arguments, ways or ideas to justify his or her own rationalization. Such attempts to try and "prove" that the Church is wrong destroys a person's spirituality; and any attempts to become closer to God is bogged down in the mire of a very deep-seated pride.

But when one has reached the heights of the prayer of Holy Abandonment, all such rationalization and chains around one's faith disappears. The person has learned and firmly believes that Christ gave to His Church the way and the means to personal sanctification. The fact is, the person has a desire to learn more about the teachings and doctrines of his or her precious Catholic Faith and finds tremendous joy when discoveries are made which had not been made before. Then the faith becomes the beacon, a brilliant light, ever shining as one walks in safety through the dark tunnel called life under the mantle of divine love lovingly extended to each soul from the Church which the person has such faith in.

It must be remembered that the Catholic Church (our Church) has had about 2000 years of experience in teaching its members how to live an active spiritual, prayer life. Such experiences extend from the very words of Christ down throughout the ages. Numerous saints left detailed instructions on how to developed a meaningful prayer life; but as they went through the different stages of their own spiritual-prayer developments, they never lost faith in the teachings of their Catholic Church; nor did they ever attempt to tell the Church that she was wrong and they were right. Their examples of love for the Church and their faith become a path to follow as a person seeks to enter into the realms of the prayer of Holy Abandonment: a path which brings with it tremendous spiritual joy and light.

GOD'S LOVE FOR THE PERSON

One of the most magnificent fruits of Holy Abandonment is the tremendous understanding which the person is blessed with concerning the love of God. It is as if Heaven itself opened before the person's spiritual eyes and the person can see, there within, the glowing Sacred Heart of Christ, glowing with an infinite love for him or her. Once this sight comes into view, never will it leave; and the person swims, as it were, in the ocean of this love for the rest of his or her life. What joy! What consolations! What a reward for a lifetime of sufferings and pain to reach such heights of union with God! There are no words to describe such a state. One can only experience it and revel in its splendor and warmth. One can then start each day and end each night with bursts of joy, hope, consolations and pure delight. One can say a thousand times a day: "God does love me," and never tire of repeating the words over and over.

This type of love experience, which the person feels, affects his deeds as well; because, never does he want to do one thing which will interfere with this love reaching his soul. There is such a delicate balance between the reception of this love by the soul and the transmission of it from its source, that great care must be taken, by the person, to keep the passageway free from all interference so that nothing will disturb the sweet notes of this divine melody. So great is the sensitivity of the person to this love that he knows immediately if there is one ounce of interference and he attempts to flee from it or correct a mistake made.

For example, if the person enters a room where there is loud, wild music playing, the person would want to flee because such music is out-of-tune with the melody of love between the soul and God. If the person must stay, such as at a party, then the person suffers greatly because he can no longer hear that melody deep within his soul. For the sweetness of the soul's love song between itself and God can only survive within the soft silence which is needed for its existence. That is why, when a person reaches the final stages of Holy Abandonment, the person seeks silence and solitude. That is why the saints always sought silence and solitude and ran away from administrative management of affairs of a convent, monastery or of a state. That is why no one, who cherishes the ways of the world and wants to gather for himself all sorts of worldly treasures and pleasures, could experience the type of love union with God which I am attempting to explain.

Now, understand that this pinnacle of union with God is not of a fanatical nature. That is very important to note. There are people who claim they "live" in God's love all the time and "prove" that by all sorts of religious activities. But all this action, which is exposed to public view, tells that they *do not* experience the type of love which I am talking about. For the main condition, by which this type of awareness of God's love for the person can develop, is within an atmosphere of silence and aloneness. God draws the soul away from worldly distractions into a state within the depths of the person's soul. Such a state could not exist with the wild activities and pride of a religious fanatic who loves to "show the world" how much he or she loves God.

In order to reach the wondrous state of living in the sunshine of God's pure love, the soul must withdraw into the inner silence where God dwells. The more the soul withdraws from material distractions into the deep silence of its inner being, the more the soul can share the secrets of God's own Heart.

Once the soul learns how to do that, then there are no reversals. The soul will never leave this type of a union with God because all else becomes cold in comparison to the warmth of God's pure love for the person. Once the fruits of God's love for the person are tasted, no other material pleasure or joy can taste as sweet. The world and all it contains becomes most undesirable; so much so, that temptations of pleasure and material joys almost completely vanish. That is the most marvelous thing about reaching the final prayer life of Holy Abandonment.

In the lower or lesser prayer stages, a soul may catch a fleeting glimpse of the type of love union with God which I am now explaining. The person may suddenly experience an overpowering feeling of God's love for him or her. The person may be touched for a moment by a dart of the piercing fire of that love; but only for a moment. Unless the soul is properly prepared to live in this high state of union with God, the soul cannot retain this fire of God's love. The soul becomes only a clumsy, awkward catcher who cannot hold onto a tossed ball. The wondrous feeling of knowing what it really means to be loved by God quickly vanishes, leaving the person's soul in a sad state. The memory lingers on but that moment cannot be recaptured simply by wishing it to return. Then the person lives almost in agony as he or she tries to remember what had been done to so experience God's love. While the person tries to relive that grand moment of spiritual joy, it may well be that his or her spiritual state worsens instead of becoming better as the result of that experience. The temptations of the material world work havoc with his or her whole spiritual life until the person begins to think that what happened never did occur at all.

Such torture and agony completely vanish once the person has been called by God into the high state of the prayer of Holy Abandonment. As I said, once the delights and sweetness of feeling, in all its fullness, God's pure love are given to such a person, then these delights do not vanish. The soul has been prepared to live in this sublime union and the soul will not leave this state. No amount of temptations can draw such a soul back into worldly amusements, distractions, sins or ways which will interfere with the soul's reception and comprehension of God's infinite love for it. The fact is, the soul can, at this point laugh at such temptations in a way that these temptations merely fall apart and lose their potency.

The soul, when actually living the prayer of Holy Abandonment, is so secure in God's love for it, that the agonies and tortures of fighting temptations disappear. No longer can the soul be tempted to find "something better" in worldly amusements, pleasures and distractions because the soul is absolutely certain that nothing better exists.

It is this freedom from doubts which becomes the difference between the soul's understanding of God's love for it found in Holy Abandonment and the soul's belief that God does love it found in lesser prayer forms. The two may, at first glance, appear to be the same. Both beliefs seem to bring the soul the same fruits. However, that is not true. In the lesser prayer forms, the soul can still be filled with doubts about God's ability to love it. This happens especially if the person had, at one time, been a great sinner. After conversion, it may take years before the person can actually believe that God does indeed love him. During these times of doubt, there can be much spiritual torture as the person is constantly tempted to lose faith in God's love for him.

Such temptations cannot appear in the last prayer stages simply because the person has no uncertainties about the fact that God does indeed love him or her with an infinite love. The person, at this point, actually holds the hand of God and will not let go. For such a soul, there is no other way to go, than to walk, hand-in-hand, with God into His Heaven of love.

One reason why this union does not disappear is that it was God, not the person, who gave this lofty state. It was God alone who called the soul into the depths of His love and then it is God alone who teaches the person the secrets of this love. So it is God who keeps the soul in this union and not the person who may want to stay in this prayer state. God will not send a soul away from this union.

In lesser or lower prayer stages, God may give to the soul a tiny taste of the sweetness of His pure love but the soul has yet to be prepared to enter a lasting union of love with Him. The person still has not overcome faults, sins, weaknesses, nor has accepted all the graces which will help him do just that. That being the case, the person still has a freedom to decide not to advance to a higher state of union with God. It is the person's own choice to accept or reject the graces necessary to do that. In that case, God cannot call the soul into the highest stages of union unless and until the person allows Him to by accepting and using all graces which lead to the prayer of Holy Abandonment. If the person does accept all such graces and has prepared his soul for the call of God into the highest stages of the prayer life, then the way is open for God to act directly and form this union with the soul. When this happens, the final step up the ladder is not within the ability of the person to take. He has prepared his soul, but he can go no higher on his own abilities. Then it is God's turn to carry the soul up to the heights which is impossible for the soul to reach by himself. And once God does carry the soul to these heights, the person will never leave them for the next and only step upward is Heaven. The soul, at this level of spirituality actually lives more in Heaven than on earth for it shares the same love with God as souls in Heaven share.

However, that does not mean that the person no longer can fulfill his daily duties and obligations. He can indeed. He can also share material joys and pleasures with his family and friends. The fact is, he will be most happy to live his material life and enjoy innocent pleasures all of which become God's holy will for him; but there will be a great difference in the way he lives his material life with all its duties, obligations, joys and pleasures. He will discover that everything in his material life must be centered around the wondrous union of love with God. As a result, he will not desire one joy or pleasure which would in any way harm his union of grace and love with God. He will not detour one inch away from his Christ-centered way of life. He will indeed find holiness most desirable as he faithfully carries out all the obligations of his daily life. He will walk away from and shun the noises and distractions which most people find attractive.

That does not mean that he will become a person filled with self-righteousness. He could not become such a person because his whole spiritual life must, of necessity, be built upon humility and grace. While he lives his Christ-centered life, his virtues of charity, goodness and kindness will make him very sensitive to the people who are in his life and to their needs.

In other words, knowing and understanding God's love for him, will make such a person want to share that love with others.

THE PERSON'S LOVE FOR GOD

Along with the love which God has for the person, there has to be, in return the person's love for God. These two loves cannot be separated. So the person's love for God becomes the *2nd* fruit of the prayer life of Holy Abandonment.

God would never call a person into the state of Holy Abandonment unless the person is capable of returning love for love. How can a person know if he is capable of loving God in a way suitable to return to God the love which the person receives from God?

The best way to know that is to prepare one's soul for the wondrous love it is to receive from God in the highest stages of union with Him. If a person has gone through years of spiritual struggles to reach the heights wherein God can call the soul into the prayer of Holy Abandonment, then that person is capable of returning love for love. The struggle is so torturous at times, the way so dark, the doubts so fierce that only a person truly in love with God can succeed in reaching the final stages of union with God.

However, as strong as such a love is, the love for God found in the prayer life of Holy Abandonment far outshines that love.

Only when a person enters into the final stages of union with God, only then can this person truly understand the full meaning of Christ's words: "You shall love the Lord, your God, with your whole heart, with your whole soul and with your whole mind" (*Matthew* 22:37).

In the lowest stages of the spiritual life, even a very strongly expressed love for God does not embrace the person's whole heart, soul and mind. That is why many a Catholic, who claims that he or she really loves God, has walked away from the sacraments into an invalid marriage when someone else, not God, becomes first in the person's heart. That is why so many people constantly use their minds to attempt to rationalize away their sins. That is why so many people give to God only empty words about their great love for Him because, at the same time, they desire something which will harm the grace within their souls. That is why many Catholics will loudly declare that they *do* love God, *yet* they will not accept some of our Church's teachings, they will not go to confession to acknowledge their own misdeeds or else they will refuse to believe a truth of God's as taught by Holy Mother Church.

All love for God which borders along those lines is far removed from the type of love which Christ tells us we must have.

As one advances up THE LADDER OF PERFECTION to a closer union with God, the love which the person has for God naturally increases and becomes more recognizable as the love which Christ described; yet, it still does not possess the quality or the perfection of the complete fulfillment of the first commandment of God. Why? Well, the person may still lack the ability to place his complete faith in his personal love for God. As a result, the person will doubt his capability to actually love God with his whole heart, mind and soul. He will often be tempted to believe that God will never accept his love; or else he will consider his love as "nothing" in the eyes of God. Even if the person becomes aware of the fact that indeed his love for God has greatly increased as he accepted and used grace, he may come to believe that it is impossible to place his love for God above all else on earth.

But when the person has actually entered into the prayer life of Holy Abandonment all such doubts, fears and personal torments about his love for God completely vanish. He knows without any doubts, that he can indeed return love for love and he can place God first in his heart, mind and soul. He knows that a mere glance of love towards God can bring all the sunshine and joy contained in loving God with his whole heart, mind and soul. He knows that his love for God soars to Heaven like the rapturous notes of an angelic melody; and he finds tremendous joy because he knows how pleased God is with this love.

A person, who has reached the prayer life of Holy Abandonment, knows that his or her love for God has been made supernatural through sanctifying grace. The person becomes completely aware of the fact that with grace, his or her love for God has become purified, so much so, that it has been washed clean of all self-interests. Also, this love is so freely given to God that the person can indeed prepare, within his or her mind, heart and soul, the place which rightfully belongs to God.

It is the total freedom of giving to God every ounce of pure love for Him, that makes this love for God so beautiful and rare. Think of the way a child gives a treasured toy to someone who has none. The child, in an act of total unselfishness, gives with his whole heart, soul and mind asking nothing in return. That is an example of total complete freedom of the will used for good without one ounce of self in this act. The child desires absolutely nothing in return for his gift which was given with pure love and even pure joy.

Unfortunately, as the person becomes older, as the person

begins to understand what he has lost when he becomes so generous, his acts of giving what he has becomes less pure and more filled with self-interests; until, he will end up not giving away anything unless he receives something in return.

In much the same way, in the spiritual life, human weaknesses and an inborn selfishness makes demands upon the person's love for God. This love is not easily given unless the person gets something in return such as spiritual consolations, gifts, favors, signs, etc. I personally believe that within the Charismatic movement the whole idea of love for the Holy Spirit is saturated with this inborn selfishness which calls for some kind of a mystical gift in exchange for all the praising of the Lord and of the Holy Spirit. This may not be a great fault in some cases of receiving the gifts of the Holy Spirit but it certainly does act as an impediment which stains the person's freedom of expressing his or her great love for God. If the person never receives a gift of the Holy Spirit, there still remains the desire to so receive one and the disappointment knowing that others seem favored with gifts, but the person is not, is somewhere hidden in the person's "praises of the Lord."

That is why people fall away so easily from the practice of their religion. The standard explanation of why a person no longer goes to Mass is: "*I* get nothing out of it." They never ask themselves: "What can I give to God by my presence at Mass?"

Also, this inborn desire or selfishness which automatically (even often without the person's full knowledge of what is happening) demands something in return for the person's love for God is the main reason why once practicing Catholics start to lose faith in God and stop loving Him.

Note also that all human love is based upon the inborn desires and demands to be loved in exchange for love given. Millions of marriages fall apart because one of the partners in the marriage feels unloved and knows that the love he or she gives is rejected and cast aside.

In the final stages of union with God, at times it may be difficult to discover what came first: the awareness of God's pure love for the soul, or the soul's pure love for God. However, *if* the person received absolutely nothing in return for his love for God, that love would still be pure, totally free, have no self-interests and it would bring the person tremendous spiritual joy. Even if the soul was completely deprived of God's love and the sunshine of that love, the person would not withdraw one ounce of his or her love for God; and would still love God with his or her whole heart, soul and mind. That is what separates the love for God found in the prayer life of Holy Abandonment from the love for God found in other stages of spiritual development.

Once this love is given to God, the person will not withdraw it. The person will desire nothing in return for this love because *this love contains all* that the person will ever want. At this stage of spiritual development, the person experiences an almost uncontrollable desire to give to others without asking anything in return. The more the soul is purified, the more unselfish the person becomes. As a result, (I will say as the first result) the person wants to do everything he can to bring joy to others. Also, this person will desire nothing in return simply because there is so much joy found in giving to others.

So, actually the person, who has reached the highest state of union with God, does not even need God's love for him or her to bring tremendous joy; because, the person finds this joy in giving pure love to God.

Along with this extraordinary, supernatural joy which the person experiences in loving God with his or her whole heart, soul and mind, there comes an equally powerful joy in being able to give to God a pure trust in Him and a love for His holy will.

One reason why the love for God, at this point of spiritual union with Him, is so pure and so freely given is that this love also expresses a total confidence in God by and through this love. The person not only becomes an unselfish person, as his or her soul is purified but all the person's virtues are purified, expanded and improved. Because of that, within this total love for God, there can be found pure faith, hope, charity, trust and so forth. As a result, the person's whole life literally becomes a life lived in inner sunshine and peace no matter what crosses or problems show themselves in daily life. The person will never fall into moods of sadness, depression or discouragement when things go wrong. The person will reveal an amazing understanding of God's will for him or her and find great delight in God's goodness and mercy, never blaming Him for whatever is not right in daily life. The person will want to gather all sorts of spiritual treasures and by-pass worldly pleasures. So, he or she will find a very great love for and joy in sufferings, penance, prayer and the sacraments. In other words, the person will be a very holy, saintly person who has the power to bring joy and comfort to others as he travels through his own daily life loving God with his whole heart, his whole soul and his whole mind.

JOY

Although the fruits of Holy Abandonment are many and diversified and each one becomes a source of immense joy, when all the fruits are gathered into one component, the most noticeable element which emerges is a joy which rises above the natural into the supernatural realm.

This joy, which I am referring to, is not a superficial type of joy or one that merely comes and goes as so often happens in the lesser spiritual stages. It is the type of joy which becomes deeply embedded within the whole personality of the one who has reached this wondrous state of spirituality. Nor is this joy one of a fanatical outburst (always guard against fanatical outbursts which usually are given for the public to see). The joy I am explaining cannot be brought forth nor felt simply by an overzealous type of love for God, such as the instant joy which makes an appearance where a person has suddenly experienced a powerful flash of "finding" Christ or the Holy Spirit. That flash of joy could very well disappear as quickly as it surfaced but not so with the joy to which I refer.

The glowing feelings of great inner happiness, which is the result of the joy of Holy Abandonment, become permanent and do not cease. The fact is, the joy expands beyond human imagination. There seems to be no limitations or boundaries to which it is contained. If, for example, the person thinks that his present joy could be no greater, he receives the surprise of discovering an increase in the wondrous jubilance. I can only explain what I mean by comparing the soul to a person who sits on the water's edge of the ocean allowing wave after wave to cover his body. When a person reaches the state of Holy Abandonment, it seems that wave after wave of joy comes upon and covers the person's whole being in a never-ending, billowing, surging motion. It is within this state where many saints found themselves caught up into holy raptures and ravishments of the soul which they found impossible to control because it was God who carried them into this "seventh Heaven" of union with Him.

It is useless for any person to attempt to produce such an ecstatic degree of pure, holy joy, no matter how much delight they personally feel in their own prayer life if the person has not advanced into the stages of Holy Abandonment. It is God alone who calls a person to such heights. No one can, of themselves through their own efforts, bring about such a condition. No amount of religious zeal or fervor could produce or imitate the spiritual condition which I am describing. No amount of fanatical religious activity could ever bring to the person the feelings of joy which the state of Holy Abandonment produces. Yet, this joy is not for public sight. It swirls deep within the silence of the soul's union with God. It will surely reveal itself in the words and actions of the person but still remain a hidden secret between the soul and God.

How can a person know if he has or has not reached the state of joy which I have just described? How can a person tell the difference between the joys in this last state of prayer and those found in other, lower degrees of prayer?

That may be difficult at first to do because there can be intense joy found in vocal prayers, mental prayers and contemplation. However, there is a striking, noticeable different uniqueness between the joys found in the state of Holy Abandonment and the joys found in the lower prayer forms. What is that unique quality? It consists of the steadfast, firm, solid, never-ending stability of the joys found in Holy Abandonment.

While it is true that one can experience overpowering moments of happiness and jubilation during all stages of prayer, only during the final stages of the prayer of Holy Abandonment do these joys linger *after* the glow of the moment disappears.

In other words, some people can become filled with feelings of joy and love for God during inspiring moments, such as when attending an exceptionally beautiful Mass or seeing a movie about a saint's great deeds; however, all too soon the coldness of reality returns with all its everyday crosses and problems. When that happens, the joys quickly fade away leaving the soul languishing in an arid condition of trying desperately to recapture the lost moment of bliss.

Such a thing never happens once the person's spiritual life has entered into the joys of Holy Abandonment. The joys therein become so much a part of the person's whole being that they are always there no matter what happens in the material life. Not only that, but there is absolutely no struggle or spiritual battle to recapture something lost because the joys never go away. Any moment of the day or night the person's whole being can explode with joy just at the mere thought or mention of the name of God.

Not only is this joy lasting but it creates a far more intimate union with the Lord than do the joys found in the lower levels of prayer. This joy actually becomes a most precious part of the person's whole prayer life. The joy, then, does not become the result of the prayer of Holy Abandonment but is actually a force within the prayer life which keeps that prayer life very, very active.

Compare the joys which emerge from any given situation which causes spiritual stimulation and the joys found in Holy Abandonment and there can be seen a most pronounced unsimilarity. They do not even resemble each other in degree or purpose. For one type, the joy which comes during the lower forms of prayer has to be a point of contact between the person receiving the joy and the object which is capable of causing such joy. For example: the person may arrive at a Mass in an unhappy, even depressed sort of mood. However, the beauty and songs which he sees and hears cause his spirits to soar high towards the God whom He loves and he becomes filled with joy. But, if there had been no Mass or beauty or songs, the person would have remained unhappy and depressed. He could not of himself rise above the depressed mood without the aid of the outside influence. All joys found in the lower stages of prayer, especially the stages of vocal prayer (the Mass, the Rosary, etc.) must come from sources outside of the person. The soul, at such levels, simply does not have the ability to produce its own joy and expand such joy outward from itself. That is why this type of joy does not last. It quickly becomes lost when the person returns to the cares and problems of his or her daily life and it can only become a memory.

However, the joys found in the final stages of the prayer of Holy Abandonment do not need any outside influence to come into being because they never cease to exist within the soul of the person. At this stage, the soul does have the capabilities to produce its own joys and does not need to rely upon inspiring events or words to find a wondrous happiness.

In other words it no longer needs words of comfort or encouragement or even love to find happiness and joy because the joy itself produces all the comfort, encouragement and love which the soul will ever need. The soul does not have to be told that God loves it, because the soul *knows* that God does indeed love and cherish it. The soul does not even need such a glorious, inspiring event as a vision of Christ to bring it joy because the soul already swims in the light of total union with Christ. His presence in vision form could not increase the soul's pure joy and happiness which it habitually possesses.

Spiritual writers teach that when the soul reaches this stage of union with God, even the joys of Heaven do not entice it because the soul is already living in the joys of Heaven and the soul knows that fact.

So, as I said, there is a vast difference between the joys found in the lower stages of prayer and the ones found in the prayer of Holy Abandonment. The joys of Holy Abandonment are so much a part of the person's spiritual life that they cause the soul to send forth a never-ending stream of praise and love for God. These joys are what stimulate the soul and lead it into prayer, rather than an outside influence which tells the soul to pray and love God because God loves the soul.

Due to that fact, such joys become very, very personal and *can-*

not be put on public view. Speaking of exposing one's personal, deep union with God and the joys of that union to the public, I cannot help but once again bring up the subject of the Charismatics. Not that I wish to constantly criticize that movement (although there is much to be criticized within it) or to downgrade the sincere people who feel they must follow that path and who do continue to live a full sacramental life; but I do find that the Charismatics offer a dandy way of showing examples for many points which I wish to elaborate. The movement is so filled with a very public sort of religious experiences that many people are lead to believe that becoming charismatic is the only way to some sort of a union with God. However, as I have already pointed out, much of the outward signs of holiness which are to be found within the movement are false and do not in any way constitute true sanctity. So also, it can be seen that much of the spontaneous outbursts of joy, exhibited by those who are involved in this movement, do not really come from a joy which can last. Here again there can be seen an example of an outward force (the crowd, the shouts of "Praise the Lord," the loud, lively songs) which must be present to produce the joys felt by those who allow themselves to be influenced by the force or power of the moment.

The true, lasting joy which comes when the highest spiritual state of union with God is reached is very personal. In spite of that, this joy can be seen by others. It reveals itself by and through the actions, words and deeds of the person so highly favored by God. However, this show of joy is never actually desired by the person who, at all times, wants to keep his wondrous union with God a secret. True sanctity and holiness are always built upon the solid foundation of true humility. That being the case, the person who has the joys of the prayer life of Holy Abandonment would prefer to live his life of joy and love for God as unnoticed as possible.

However, the examples which are shown by this person, as he lives his religion in his daily life, cannot remain hidden. These examples (*not public* outburst of joy) become the silent witnesses of grace, love and joy within the person's soul; which are seen and often admired by others.

The first example to be seen is to take note of the fact that a person who has reached the heights of union with God lives a life of joy, at all times, no matter what events take place. It is true that the person can cry at times or become upset; however, the inner joy and peace of soul will not vanish.

PRAYER

Another wondrous fruit found only in the prayer life of Holy Abandonment concerns prayer itself. I have already explained about vocal prayers, mental prayer and contemplative prayer. The prayer found in Holy Abandonment embraces all three forms of prayer, which by this time the person is very familiar with. Actually these three types of prayer, which become a vital part of any spiritual life, are all that is needed to live a very deep, active prayer life. So why would it be necessary to say that in the prayer life of Holy Abandonment there is an added fruit called prayer? Is not the whole spiritual life a prayer life?

The answer to those questions lies within the understanding of the methods used for prayer. In the first method, vocal prayer, the person must read or say certain prayers, whether the prayer is the Rosary, the Our Father, the Mass or merely words which the person composed himself. In the second method, mental prayer, the person must find a regular time in which to meditate. The person must also form in his mind mental pictures so that he can meditate upon a certain subject. In the third form, contemplation, the person has to find a time and a place to relax (such as in an empty Church) and raise the mind and heart to God so that God can draw this soul closer to Him.

Note that in all three methods of prayer, the person must do something before he can enter into each form of prayer. The person must say or read vocal prayers, the person must form mental pictures in his mind to meditate and the person must place himself into an atmosphere of contemplation so that God can draw the soul into depths of His love.

With the prayer of Holy Abandonment, there is a most striking and noticeable difference. While the lesser forms of prayer life do bring much grace and union with God, the three different forms of prayer life have a beginning and an ending. That is not true with the prayer of Holy Abandonment. This prayer has no beginning or ending. While it incorporates within itself the standard prayers of vocal, mental and contemplative, the prayer of Holy Abandonment never ceases. It becomes perpetual; so much so, that all the person's deeds, thoughts and actions become an unending prayer of love to God because everything the person does, thinks or accomplishes is so in tune with God's holy will. That is one of the most wondrous fruits of the prayer of Holy Abandonment. This fruit becomes more desirable when it is seen that the offshoots of the prayer of Holy Abandonment produce a very stabilizing force within which the problems found in other forms of prayer completely disappear.

And these problems do plague, in various degrees, all other forms of prayer. The first and most common problem associated with prayer is the inability to actually get down to the business of praying. Especially in the lower forms of prayer, the person knows that it is really a struggle to find time to say the Rosary, to go to Mass or to meditate. There is always the constant battle which comes (in various degrees with different people) when the person wants to turn off the world and tune into God's Heaven by means of prayer.

Many other problems surface in lesser forms of prayer which are absent in the highest form called Holy Abandonment. Very often, within lower spiritual states, the prayers which people say are very dry, dull and often meaningless. A person may, for years, recite prayers, go to Mass and say the Rosary in only a mechanical sort of way without expressions or feelings of love. They, more or less, pray because this has become a habit instead of being prompted to pray because of love for God and Mary.

Another serious and common problem of the prayer life in the lesser stages of spirituality are numerous distractions. Often a person can attend a Mass and later not remember anything that had happened during Mass because his or her mind was "a million miles" away.

Another very serious problem, which is commonly found in the lesser stages of the prayer life, is the temptation to give up prayer altogether. Many times this temptation wins and the person will say: " I cannot pray anymore."

Then there is the person's own departure from prayer because he has lost faith in God and can no longer trust Him. To such a person, the logical solution is to merely stop praying.

Finally, there is the person who wants to "punish" God by not praying because God did not answer the person's prayer or allowed a tragedy in the person's life, such as the death of a loved one.

All such problems and others related to these situations disappear when the person has entered into the highest form of prayer called Holy Abandonment.

How can that happen? Well, because the person then is *living* the prayer life as well as actually praying on his or her knees.

To *live* a prayer life is far different than to merely *say* prayers. It is this part about actually living a total, complete prayer life which becomes the main difference between the prayer life of Holy Abandonment and the lesser prayer forms.

What exactly does that mean, to live the prayer life? It means, not only to pray with set prayers at an appointed time, but to make everything you do a prayer of love to God. How can a person do such a thing? First of all, by doing nothing that will displease God. Once a person is so in tune with God's holy will, that person will desire nothing which would become for him or her a sin. When such a state is reached, this love for God's holy will along with a true aversion for sin turns a person's whole day into one of constant praise for God; because, all that the person does is done with God, for God and for the good of the person's own soul. Prayer in itself brings a soul into union with God. That being the case such a holy life becomes a never-ending prayer of love for God.

Once this union is reached, the person's soul finds great delight in knowing that his or her whole life is a prayer of love for God. As a result, no temptation will make him or her do something that would cause this constant prayer to cease. The person will instead want to increase his or her prayer life. How can that be done? By and through the regular prayer forms. For example, the person will find great joy going to Mass, saying the Rosary, reading holy books and the Bible. He or she will look forward, with great longings, to receiving the Lord in Holy Communion. Trust and faith in God will increase beyond human imagination. Every word uttered in vocal prayer will be filled with expressions of pure love for God and each word will be most meaningful. The person will tell God how much he or she loves Him; even if prayers are not answered.

In other words, the person will find and understand the main purpose of prayer which is to love and worship God, to praise Him and to be united with Him. At this point, all prayer becomes a source of great joy, never dull, never lifeless, never meaningless.

The person will also find it very, very easy to raise his or her heart and mind to God at any given moment in daily life. Because he or she enjoys such an intimate relationship with God, the person lives constantly in the presence of God. That being the case, the person actually lives within the light of Heaven.

When a person has reached this state of the spiritual life in which he or she experiences the light and love of God every moment of every day, the person is actually living more in Heaven than on earth. The sweet fruits of Heaven are there to taste and savor. Once tasted, never will he she step backward into a world of material pleasures and desires. So, never can such things distract the mind or prayer life. This, then, becomes the prayer found in Holy Abandonment.

AWARENESS OF SIN

Another wondrous fruit of the prayer of Holy Abandonment is to have a very sharp, keen awareness of sin. This awareness actually prevents the person from committing even a small venial sin and causes the person to suffer intensely because of even a slight fault. It is this fruit of awareness which prompted the saints to do severe penances for all their "sins" when in reality such sins were only slight faults caused by human weakness. Such strong self-punishment may seem excessive and unnecessary to an untrained eye; however, when a person understands the awareness of sin which the saints had, then they can see the reason why the saints did what they did for penance.

In this state of total abandonment to God's holy will, they knew what malice even a small fault can have towards the goodness and love of God. If they did fall into a slight fault, they instantly wanted to do penance so that this act of penance would make up for the malice.

Now, do not mistake this awareness of sin for scruples. Scruples occur when an innocent person suffers agony because he thinks he has committed "horrible" sins when in reality he has not. Such a person believes that no matter what he does or has done "everything" is a sin. The agony of scruples becomes a great stumbling block within the person's spiritual life. It is a spiritual illness which has to be cured before any advancement can be made towards closer union with God.

There is a tremendous difference between scruples and the awareness of sin which comes within the life of Holy Abandonment. With scruples, the person's concept of God's love for him is as clouded as his understanding of faults and sins. As a result, the person's main agony, suffered because of scruples, also involves a feeling of rejection by God as well as imagining that he is the greatest sinner on earth.

There are no such feelings of rejection by a person who has reached the final stages of Holy Abandonment. The fact is, the person is so aware of God's love for him that he suffers, not from any feelings of rejection as do the people who suffer from scruples and sins which do not even exist, but from the fact that the sin is a sign of the person's refusal to give to God the love which God deserves.

At this high point in the person's prayer life, not only is he completely aware of the malice of even a tiny sin, but he is also completely aware of what sin actually is and what even a small sin can do to God. The person so understands God's love for him and his love for God that even a small fault becomes for him a refusal to give to God his complete love and obedience. It acts as a barrier to the smooth flow of love between God and the soul, the exchange of love for love. Because the person's one desire is to give every ounce of his or her love and obedience to God, even a small fault or sin must be corrected at once.

The eraser used to blot out the stain is called penance. One of the most important differences between a person suffering from scruples and someone who has entered into the prayer life of Holy Abandonment and thus has a keen awareness of sin is the person's love for penance. Such a love is completely lacking in someone who suffers from scruples even if the person wants to "punish" himself for his "horrible" sins. This self-punishment is not true penance and there is no joy in it.

But there is a very great joy found in penance by a saintly person who has received the spiritual insight of a true awareness of the malice of sin. Such a person is so on guard for signs of sins and faults that he instantly becomes aware of them no matter how small they are. As a result, he instantly wants to do a penance for the slightest offenses; and he finds great joy knowing that there is this way to make amends.

Note also this difference between a person who has entered into the highest form of prayer life and someone who might still be in the lower or lesser forms in regard to the awareness of sin.

Very often a person in the lower prayer forms overlooks faults, weaknesses and slight sins which to him or her may not even seem to be wrong. For example, many people are guilty of telling "little, white" lies, of cheating "just a little bit," of spreading unkind gossip, of displaying many signs of anger or impatience, etc. While these little faults and sins (venial sins) may not bother the person and do not have to be confessed, a person who is living the life of Holy Abandonment would consider such misdeeds as interfering with the love union between himself or herself and God.

In such a person's mind, a sin is still a sin no matter how slight it is, a fault is still a fault which must be corrected, a tiny rejection of an actual grace must be acknowledged and a penance must be done. So clearly does this person see misdeeds or rejections of actual grace that he or she, in essence, judges them as God would, not as a human being would. The person is so close to the sunlight of God's ways that nothing escapes his or her attention, for all is seen as it really is and not hidden behind the darkness of human rationalization and spiritual blindness.

TEMPTATIONS

Another wondrous fruit, which comes when a person is called by God into the highest prayer life of Holy Abandonment, concerns temptations or rather the lack of temptations. At this high level of spirituality, the person may still be tempted; however, most severe temptations simply fade away and never return. The reason being, the devil cannot come near enough with his enticements to cause the person agonizing temptations.

This does not mean that the person will no longer suffer because of human failings and weaknesses. But there is a decisive difference between these sufferings and the ones caused by hammering temptations.

With the temptations, the agony and torments come before an act of sin is committed or rejected. When the person has reached the heights of Holy Abandonment, the suffering comes only after a slight fault reveals the person's human weaknesses. Actually, no human being can become totally free from all human weaknesses simply because the person still remains a human being even if he lives on a supernatural level of existence. The fact is, God may leave in the person some traces of human weakness as a reminder, to the person, that all his strength comes from God and grace.

However, as for torturous temptations, they become a thing of the past for someone who experiences the lofty heights of Holy Abandonment. The person's whole being is so consumed by his or her love-for-love union with God, that the devil knows it is useless to actually tempt the person to fall into life's most common, serious sins.

However, that does not mean that the devil completely vanishes from the picture. He is still ready, willing and able to attempt to trick the person into being unfaithful to grace. He changes his methods radically but never his reasons, which are always to win a soul for his Hell.

The most extreme change which the devil makes is to cleverly allow the person freedom to merely walk into his own faults and human weaknesses without any violent temptations and then to let the person's own guilt cause his sufferings. In other words, he allows the person's own reactions, after a slight fall, to lead (he hopes) into depression and discouragement. If that happens, then he can pounce upon the person with more formal temptations. Yet, the truth of the matter is that the depression and discouragement never materialize.

The person is so close to the perfect fulfillment of all efforts, which is to be found in total union with God in Heaven, that he or she does not waste precious thought-time becoming discouraged or depressed because of a slight fall. Also, there is such joy in penance that the person constantly looks for opportunities to do all sorts of penance even if he or she does not commit a personal fault. The person knows that penance is not only a way to purify the soul, but also a way to help save souls and to help the souls in Purgatory. With such noble motivations, the soul is protected from the traps of the devil which could lead it into any type of self-destruction.

However, the devil does not give up completely his quest for the person's vulnerabilities. He begins to try to win the soul by and through the person's loved ones and friends.

The most common method used by the devil for this purpose is to have a loved one complain about the person's holiness. If the husband has reached a high state of union with God, for example, the wife may object to this and call him a holier-than-thou sort of person. Or it could be reversed and the husband may not understand the spiritual life which the wife is living. In addition, other members of the family and close friends may bring sufferings to the person by cruel remarks about his love for God and for virtue. All the while, such remarks are used by the devil to try and destroy the person's union with God.

Naturally the person becomes very hurt by such remarks and is greatly bothered by them. However, his union with God, at this point, is so complete that he has a marvelous gift of wisdom. He can see, very clearly, the devil's use of others to try to destroy his precious spiritual life. Far from giving up his prayer life, the cruel remarks only make him pray more; this time for the very ones who are causing his suffering. He is, indirectly, telling the devil that the more the devil uses others to try to destroy his union with

God, the more he will pray to convert these people who may not be living an active spiritual life.

Please note that I am *not* saying that the people making the unkind remarks are with the devil. They are merely being used by the devil who cleverly creates situations wherein they find reasons to downgrade the virtues and holiness of the recipient of such cruel remarks. They do not know they are being manipulated in such a way by the devil, so they, unknowingly, completely cooperate with the ways the devil attempts to use them.

Once again, I am not talking about religious fanatics. I am speaking about a person who has a high degree of sanctity and who lives a beautiful, holy, spiritual life. If the person is a fanatic, then the complains about his religious activities are justified.

Very often the spiritual person may be harassed by his friends and members of his family for years. Yet, he continues to live a very close union with God. The more the persons suffers, the more his love for God and his spiritual life are strengthened. Often God uses this method to further purify the person's soul for an even closer union with Him. Through it all, the person, although he can be deeply hurt by cruel remarks, remains calm and always forgiving.

Many times only a great tragedy, such as the sudden death of a loved one, reveals the magnificent spiritual strength of the one who lives in high union with God. Then his examples shine forth for others to see. As a result, it often happens, that the person causing him the most problems, because of his spiritual life, will be converted due to the way these examples affect him or her. Then the devil lost the battle and all his efforts were useless.

Another trick which the devil employs to try and destroy the person's high state of union with God is to have the people, friends and relatives, who are closest to his heart, turn against him. Sometimes, the once close friend or relative will completely disown him, and for no apparent reason. This type of hurt is far worse than the sufferings brought about because of cruel, unkind remarks.

A loss of a close friendship can become so heavy a cross to

carry, for the person, that he could be tempted to say to God: "After all I did for you, you allow this to happen to me!" However, when a person lives a life of Holy Abandonment, that person has truly placed God first in his life. As a result, he cannot be tempted to turn against God simply because his love for God and God's love for him is so precious to him. He has the wisdom to understand that the only love and affection that are eternal belong only to the eternal God. While he is sad because of the loss of a dear friend or relative, in such a way, he knows that he still has the most perfect love on earth, which is far greater than any which can come from a human heart.

It is very important to know that anyone, who has in truth reached the spiritual heights of Holy Abandonment, has the grace necessary to fully understand that a person's desires for a lasting, pure, infinite love and affection can only be realized within the heart of the infinite God. While lost or broken friendships and relationships on earth can deeply hurt the person, the devil cannot destroy the person's union with God through such means because the person still lives within the wondrous light of God's love. Unlike someone who builds his or her whole life around the love of another human being, the person on the spiritual level of the highest union with God builds his whole life around the unchanging love of God. In that case, no loss of a human's love and affection can throw the person into a state of depression. The fact is, the loss of a human's love and affection only makes being closer to God and His love more desirable because God shares His infinite love with the person.

CLARITY

One of the most extraordinary and unique fruits of Holy Abandonment is the clarity or clearness with which the person, who lives this high life of union with God, can view all things. The person sees, as if he looks through the eyes of God, and understands with a comprehension fashioned by the gifts of the Holy Spirit. It is as though a heavy, thick veil has been lifted from the person's eyes and intellect. He can observe his own life, the lives of the people who surround him and even events in the world filled with a wisdom which other people do not possess. How is this possible?

It must be remembered that some of the gifts of the Holy Spirit are knowledge, wisdom and understanding. As the person grows in grace, so do these virtues grow and expand. When the person has reached the final stages of Holy Abandonment, these virtues shine forth in all their radiance.

To explain more fully what I mean, think of how dull a conscience can become when deprived of grace and the gifts of the Holy Spirit. Someone who has fallen away from the sacraments can reach the low point wherein sin no longer seems wrong to the person. He can then turn against God and the Church and tell himself that God, His Church and all the commandments are wrong, while he remains "perfect" no matter what he does. Such a person is living a lie and cannot see the way God and virtue must be part of a daily life. On the other hand, the more grace a person has, the more virtue and gifts of the Holy Spirit he possesses, the more clearly does he see and understand the reasons why God, virtue and grace must become a part of his daily life.

In much the same way, a person who has lost the grace of God through mortal sin, has also lost the virtue of wisdom which comes with sanctifying grace. Such a person becomes not only blind to the malice of his own sins, but, in addition, he finds it difficult to understand the ways of God. He is the first person to complain about the least cross he is asked to carry. He will loudly shout: "If there is a God, why do so many people have to suffer?" He believes that nothing good exists in the world and he thinks that he is the only one on earth who does things correctly.

Now compare such a person to a fallen sinner who has been touched by grace and has been converted. If this conversion is sincere and lasting, this person will develop an amazing wisdom and clarity concerning God and His ways. The more grace he or she receives and uses, the more clearly will he or she understand the God whom the person has grown to love so dearly and the ways of God.

The more one grows in the Spirit and likeness of Christ, the more the person is able to think as Christ thinks, to see as Christ sees and to understand as Christ understands. The more the person empties the inner being of spiritual blindness, the more the person takes upon himself or herself the nature of God which enables the person to more closely imitate God's own wisdom.

As a result, such a person will never question God's holy will when God gives a cross to carry. The person will know that much suffering found within humanity is caused, not by God, but as a result of man's mistakes, sins and wrongdoings. The person understands the gentle, tender mercy of God towards all of His children as He stands by their side to help them carry such crosses. The person not only understands the mercy of God, but His justice as well.

The person constantly sees goodness in other people and becomes edified when these people live as God wants them to live. The person finds all the natural beauty in the world which God gives to man for his comfort and enjoyment. He sees the hand of God touch the mountains, fields, flowers, oceans, birds and animals with a splendor of goodness and loveliness.

Now take all such examples of the virtue of wisdom which comes with sanctifying grace and multiply them a thousandfold and you will have some idea of the wisdom which a person has when he has reached the heights of union with God called Holy Abandonment.

That is mainly why the ordinary person seeks out a holy, saintly man to listen to his words of wisdom. That is why the saints displayed miraculous feats of wisdom in all sorts of matters.

The person who has reached the heights of Holy Abandonment knows, without any doubts, what it means to act, think and do as if Christ Himself were there acting, thinking and doing in his stead.

Before I leave this part about the fruit of clarity, I cannot help but record these words which come from (*Proverbs* 2:1-9): "My son, if you receive my words and treasure my commands, turning your ear to wisdom, inclining your heart to understanding; yes, if you call to intelligence, and to understanding, raise your voice. Then search out wisdom like a hidden treasure. You will then understand the fear of the Lord; the knowledge of God you will find. For the Lord gives wisdom. . .knowledge and understanding. Then you will understand rectitude and justice, honesty, every good path."

CARRYING CROSSES

One of the most puzzling spiritual problems which I have discovered most everyone has, even those who have reached a high level of spirituality, is the inability to carry crosses. Time after time I have seen people's spiritual lives completely fall apart when a heavy sorrow enters their lives. Very often a person loves God dearly, goes to the sacraments faithfully until a loved one dies. Then this person "punishes" God for this cross by no longer loving Him, praying to Him or going to Mass.

It seems that in many cases, the strength or desire to carry crosses is very much lacking in spiritual lives. As a result, the person lives in union with God only when days are filled with sunshine and joy. Or else the person expects to be rewarded with a perfect life of joy and happiness for his or her faith.

There are many Catholics who consider themselves good Catholics, yet who will leave their Church and the sacraments to find a false happiness in an invalid marriage. They seem to imagine that this happiness "proves" that God is "on their side." They are under the impression that happiness leads to salvation instead of grace.

However, that is not true. Christ meant it when He said: "Take up your cross and follow me" (*Matthew* 16:24).

As a person journeys through the different stages of the prayer life, one thing he has to face constantly is the cross. If he wants to be in union with Christ, he must also be in union with the cross of Christ. While he may not be in love with this cross, he must acknowledge it and know that upon his own cross will he be made ready to rise with Christ on the day of resurrection.

In the early or lesser prayer stages, crosses become great barriers which hinder spiritual advancement. Most people never rise higher than the lowest levels of spirituality simply because there is the obstruction of some cross.

Many others who do want to climb higher up THE LADDER OF

PERFECTION become discouraged because of the sufferings and crosses found on the spiritual battlefields.

Other people believe that God "punishes" them with crosses, when in reality He only tries to teach them lessons.

There are numerous examples of the way people try to run away from problems and crosses because they are afraid to face them.

However, when a person enters into the prayer life of Holy Abandonment, crosses do not cause the problems I have just explained. Such a person not only understands crosses, but finds a spiritual joy carrying them for the love of God; so much so, that he or she would actually miss crosses if these crosses were removed from his or her life.

When the person has entered into the highest prayer life, the person knows and understands the hidden treasures found in crosses.

The person also experiences a most profound result of these crosses within the spiritual life which others who are in the lower forms of spirituality cannot encounter. The person actually can feel the soul being purified by suffering and crosses.

To the person, this is a most wondrous grace from God. He or she rejoices in this purification in much the same way that the souls in Purgatory rejoice because they are given the means to take away the punishment due for their sins. Consequently, crosses are regarded as being most beneficial and used as penance to take away the temporal punishment due for sins. This is one reason why the saints looked for every opportunity to do penance. They could actually feel the spiritual value of penance and sufferings within their own souls.

That does not mean that the person no longer suffers pain or heartache because of crosses. He or she is still a human being with human feelings. However, the more the person suffers, the greater is faith because he or she knows that only through the darkness of the cross can there be seen the price paid for man's sins. That fact keeps thoughts about suffering in the correct perspective. In other words, the person fully understands *why* there has to be suffering and crosses; because there is no other way for man to know the seriousness of his own sins. As a result of this insight, the person who has reached the heights of the prayer life of Holy Abandonment understands fully what it means to be not only united with Christ but with the crucified Christ as well. Saint Paul put this truth so well in these words: "With Christ, I am nailed to the cross" (*Galatians* 2:19).

So, by the time the person has followed Christ up the hill of Calvary, that person is ready to die upon the cross which tortured the body of our Lord. He or she never forgets that the cross was used for his or her personal salvation by the beloved Redeemer.

So many people, who live a lesser spiritual life in the lower forms of prayer, constantly look for a Christ who comes to them without His cross. So we find among this vast number of Christians the ones who look only for Christ the teacher or Christ the healer or Christ the brother. When they get near to Christ the crucified one, they tend to stop the spiritual advancement which led them into the shadow of that cross.

For those who are not willing to pay the price for personal sanctification, it is the first heavy cross laid upon their shoulders which causes them to rebel and give up.

However, for a person who has reached the prayer stages of Holy Abandonment, this could never happen. Gladly does such a person accept and love the crosses which the good Lord places upon his shoulders. Never does he rebel against them. With grace and the wisdom, of which I have already spoken, the person understands crosses and knows their value.

SPIRITUAL DETACHMENT

For the valorous few who are called to enter into the spiritual prayer life of Holy Abandonment, a fruit which can almost be called unexpected presents itself. It is a wondrous spiritual peace which comes by way of detachment from the material world and all its pleasures. Actually this peace envelops the whole prayer state, however, this peace becomes more deeply felt or profound when it is placed within the environment of spiritual detachment. The reason being that the more a person detaches himself or herself from the fickle, changing joys, pleasures and interests of the material world, the more his or her inner being is empty of self. When this inner being becomes empty of self, then Christ, with His peace and joys, fills the void. The less noises of the material world that are heard, the more profound the peace of Christ becomes within the silence of detachment.

Often the soul does not even fully realize how truly detached it has become from all material ways and interests until it begins to experience the peace or quietude, as it is sometimes called, which is a sure sign that the detachment has indeed taken place.

The detachment of which I speak must not be confused with interior mortification. That is a virtue used to change thoughts from useless ones into spiritual innovations. Detachment is not a virtue but a way of living the spiritual life.

The best way to describe detachment is to explain what attachment is all about. First of all, please know that I am not talking about *necessary* occupations or objects in your state of life. With the virtue of interior mortification, I was talking about using that method to pry out of your mind *useless* thoughts, ideas or desires and *unnecessary* daydreams.

Let us take an even closer look at a person's daily life and see not only how it can be crowded with useless deeds, actions, thoughts, conversations, entertainments, daydreams and such; but how much time and thought are consumed, during one day, as the person carries out *necessary* duties and occupations.

If the person is a busy mother or father or lay person, who does have such responsibilities as raising children, no matter what the person does to earn a living or to take care of certain duties and obligations, many things are always needed. These consist of a home, a place to live, clothes, money to buy what is needed, food, entertainment, etc. These are life's necessities. Add to that list, plans for an education, building a new home, buying a new car, having a social life, planning a vacation, and so forth. Please note that I am not talking about religious duties and obligations, which remain very important in one's daily life. What I am talking about are the necessary things which we all need in order to live a life upon our level of personal achievement. There is nothing wrong with working hard to improve one's state of life or merely to "keep things going." But what can be wrong for someone who wants to live a high state of spirituality is to become overly attached to what is part of one's daily life. In other words, a person can develop a very great love for material objects which he or she feels life would be empty without. This attachment becomes the breeding ground for vices and sins such as greed, selfishness and jealousy. Too much attachment to or desire for what is known as the "good life" has been the motive for numerous crimes as well as sins: embezzlement, murder, stealing, kidnapping, and so forth.

The true Christian attitude about material possessions or a way of life is to become satisfied with whatever one has, not to be jealous of what others have and to thank God for His goodness to the person, even if the person has very little in the way of material possessions.

Detachment reaches beyond the limits of ordinary Christian satisfaction with one's life and what is in that life into the areas of spiritual separation of one's heart from even the legitimate pleasures, delights, plans, and desires of one's way of life. This type of detachment is a voluntary act based upon the use of grace so as to reach a more personal, purer union with God.

Before I say more about this subject, please note that I *am not* telling you to sell all you have and leave the daily duties of your life. The whole purpose of this book is to teach you how to find holiness and a close union with God within your own daily life. So, do not think that you cannot possess whatever you feel is needed or you can afford in your state of life; for you can. If you must have and can afford many material objects to maintain your and your family's social position, you need not feel guilty because of that.

However, to require material objects, to be able to afford to buy them in one thing. To be spiritually detached from them, when you possess them, is another matter altogether.

Now, what exactly is spiritual detachment? First of all, I will explain what it is not. It is not a morbid or unhealthy attitude towards life and material possessions which makes a person condemn these possessions, laughter, innocent good times or working to improve one's state of life. It is not a fanatical outburst of "I don't care about anything in my life." It is not a strict, rigorous, scrupulous, disciplinary, stern, harsh viewpoint in regards to the acquisition of material possessions. It is a deeply spiritual, inner disposition which enables the person to look at all things in his or her life as a gift from God which belong more to Him than to the person.

A good example of what I mean is contained in these words spoken by a mother of a large family: "My children are not really mine, but God's. He gave them to me for a short time, and I am to, one day, give them back to Him." In like manner, if you can take a good look at your life and see it as only a temporary arrangement given to you by God wherein you can save and sanctify your soul, if you can place God in the center of your life and know that He is first in your heart, mind and soul, then you have spiritual detachment. But that is only the beginning of detachment. If you can say that everything is fine and dandy when your dreams come true and you get what you want; then, if you can continue to say that everything is all right when a dream does not come true, you will be practicing the detachment found in Holy Abandonment. This is not an attitude of "I don't care," but one of "I don't mind because I so love God's holy will."

It is the pure love for God's holy will which makes detachment so beautiful and so filled with peace. You must remember that God's holy will is not always one which brings sorrow, sadness or tears. It is also God's holy will to have you find much joy and happiness in your life. The idea is to accept all: crosses, sorrows and joys as a gift from God to you.

Detachment means to be attached to God's holy will and His love instead of being attached to life on earth and all it offers in the way of material possessions, happiness and pleasures. It means to acknowledge God as the giver of whatever you possess in the way of material possessions, innocent pleasures and dreams-come-true; and to allow Him to take back what He no longer wishes you to have.

A good example of a person who has true spiritual detachment is the following. This person has a beautiful material life filled with all sorts of pleasures and joys. In addition, this person is fairly religious and has a personal union with God. Suddenly, his beloved wife dies and much of life's innocent joys and pleasures die with her. Many people who have to face such a situation immediately turn away from God by saying: "If you really loved me, you would never have allowed such a thing to happen to me." However, a person who has true detachment will look at God with tears streaming down his face and say: "Dearest God, I accept and love your holy will; and I thank you for the precious moments of joy which you have allowed me to spend on earth with my beloved wife."

In other words, a person who has true detachment will understand that life changes, that it is far from stable. What is good today in one's life may be changed to something bad tomorrow.

A person, who has spiritual detachment, may one day experience great joy and happiness within his or her material life and the next day experience great sadness and sorrow; yet, this person never once turns away from union with God because of the events in daily life. For this person has placed the source of his or her greatest joy and happiness *in* God's love and *not* in the circumstances of daily life.

There are numerous people who search for a lasting, infinite happiness and joy in material objects or in fickle human relationships. These people are constantly being disappointed and plunged into the darkness of despair. They seek to find their "Garden of Eden" on earth and never does their impossible quest end. All the while they long for, search for and fail to find a lasting contentment and enchantment in material objects or finite relationships, they overlook the love which God has for them: this love which remains the only unchanging safe harbor for their desires and hopes.

A person who has the graces to practice spiritual detachment in his or her daily life cannot help but be a happy, contented person. For this person looks beyond the horizons of life on earth and clearly sees the eternal joys of Heaven. All things concerned with material joys, happiness and pleasure are put into the correct perspective. He does not jeopardize his personal peace, joy and happiness by placing them within the confines of limited, changeable material events, possessions or circumstances.

This does not mean that one cannot enjoy material pleasures or innocent forms of amusement. This does not mean that he or she cannot find happiness within all the good things in life; such as, family, work, hobbies. What it means is that when material pleasures, joys and happiness are taken away, the person will still possess the wondrous peace, joys and happiness which are to be found deep within the heart of God.

Another good example of what true spiritual detachment produces within the person's union with God is seen when a person is able to overcome attachments which seem, at first glance, to be insignificant. If the person has an attachment to a certain kind of clothing, music, food or place of amusement, this may not seem very important. But when this person has reached the prayer life of Holy Abandonment grace tells him or her that in some way, no matter how slight, these attachments become imperfections and could hinder spiritual advancement. So he or she learns how to become detached from them by means of sacrifice and inner mortifications. The person finds a great, powerful aid, which helps the practice of spiritual detachment in these matters, by and through charity. To conquer these imperfections, the person loves to give to others the objects which are dear to his or her own heart or to refuse to buy them and to give the money he or she would have spent to the Church or to the poor. This type of charity is a must especially if the person can well afford to buy the things which are the most desirable.

It is this art of spiritual detachment that is so clearly seen in the lives of the saints who found such great joy in giving to others. Often a saint would give away his own clothing or food to someone who had less than he had, or nothing at all.

Also, because spiritual detachment is so important in living a very active spiritual life, all religious take a vow of poverty. This vow does not mean that they must starve or freeze in winter with no shelter or proper clothing. It means that the nun, priest or brother cannot attach his or her heart to any material possession.

Lay people do not have to take a vow of poverty, but the

Church teaches them the value of fasting, penance and sacrifice for the good of their own souls. All such acts help to teach them the true value and necessity of spiritual detachment.

Spiritual detachment, then, has to be found in its purest forms within the prayer life of Holy Abandonment. However, by the time this state of prayer life is reached spiritual detachment becomes more or less effortless. When the soul experiences the joys of pure love for God, it cares little about material pleasures, comforts and even joys. Nothing on earth can be compared to the wondrous lights which fill the soul when it has emptied itself of all material attachment so as to make room for the love of God; and the soul will not retreat from this haven of joy, happiness and peace.

LASTING PEACE

I saved this precious fruit of Holy Abandonment for the end of this chapter; because, in a sense, it does become the end result of living the prayer life of Holy Abandonment. Yet, it is not strictly the end result because this type of peace permeates the whole of an active spiritual life. But there is a difference between the peace found within the prayer life of Holy Abandonment. The one difference is that this peace is lasting; whereas, the peace found in other prayer lives becomes most unsteady: now you have it, now you don't.

I think that one of the things which disturb those who want to climb THE LADDER OF PERFECTION the most is the fact that sometimes they found the most wondrous peace deep within their beings and then suddenly it was gone! How they longed to recapture it! They cannot forget the joys which that peace brought; then, they cannot get accustomed to the sudden emptiness which developed in their souls when it disappeared.

There is a vast difference between people who never once experienced this tremendous spiritual peace and those who had, then lost it. The ones who never tasted the sweetness of this inner tranquillity cannot realize that something very precious is missing from their daily lives. The ones who had this peace and then lost it, never stop longing to recapture what left a void deep within their spiritual lives when it vanished. This empty chasm cannot be filled by any other feeling, emotion or spiritual consolation. There is no substitute for it. Nothing is like it nor can anything else imitate its sweetness and desirability.

Many times people have come to me trying to explain that once they had experienced a great peace within their beings, and it vanished; yet, never have they stopped longing to recapture what they lost. Sometimes a person may have lived for many years without this peace, still he or she cannot forget the feeling of joy which it brought. Often there had been only a fleeting touch of peace upon the soul, but the memory of all its gentle warmth and sweetness remained.

The expressions: "God was so very near to me" or "I felt like an innocent child so loved by God" or "I felt as if I were in Heaven then I had to come back to this cold earth" are common when one tries to explain the wondrous peace which I am referring to.

Now, just exactly what is this peace, how is it obtained, how is it lost?

The best say to understand what this peace consists of is to know the opposite. A person, who is filled with doubts, fears, inner conflicts, turmoils, feelings of guilt, and so forth, cannot create within himself the foundation which is necessary for this peace to rest upon. A person, who refuses to leave the material noises of the world likewise cannot taste the sweetness of the inner peace which I am talking about. A person, who is a religious fanatic, also could never taste the sweet-honey harmony of this peace. A person who refuses to acknowledge and correct his or her sins, faults and weaknesses cannot possess this peace. Why?

First of all, this peace is not a self-made state of inner quietude. No one could ever create this peace within his or her own being. It is a gift from God, the Holy Spirit, and becomes a result of living a life of prayer, holiness and virtue.

In one way, I do not like to use the word result; however, that is what it becomes. This peace can only be found, in all its lasting fullness, at the top of THE LADDER OF PERFECTION. It can only be part of a person's complete union with God. The fact is, this peace becomes one of the motivating forces which enables a person to keep struggling up that ladder. That is one reason why a person can experience slight samples of this profound spiritual stillness as he passes through lower prayer stages. God sends such moments of consolations to entice and attract the soul in a way that will encourage the soul to defeat all the obstacles which stand in the way of its advancement into the highest state of union with Him. Then, and only then, can the soul actually swim in the celestial waters of this peace, and never fear that this peace will disappear.

The main reason why people "lose" the feeling of intense spiritual well-being, if they had had a taste of its desirability, is that they do not know that the lasting peace which they so long for can only be found at the top of THE LADDER OF PERFECTION. As a result of this lack of knowledge, they place this peace within their own actions as emerging from something which they did for God. Because they will suddenly be submerged into this peace while praying or doing something for God, they believe that the only way to constantly live within this spiritual state is to do exactly what was being done when God allowed a touch of peace to descend upon their souls.

This knowledge or belief could very easily *destroy* a person's whole spiritual life when the person becomes fanatical about religious duties and obligations and increases his or her actions in this field. Such a person will increase prayers and devotions to the point of disrupting his or her whole material life in order to find what was lost. Most of these religious fanatics will say that they are "happy" or "at peace" only when they work feverishly for the Lord. They may believe that indeed outward signs and activities of a religious nature bring them the peace which they so desire. However, such a feeling of peace is not the type of peace I am talking about.

Anyone sinner, saint or religious fanatic can, at times, possess a certain amount of inner peace and feelings of personal satisfactions such as: "All is well, nothing bothers me." Sometimes sinners will even believe that God "answered" their prayers when material events bring them the forbidden, illicit pleasures, joys and material gains which they felt they could not live without. For example: many people, who lived through a valid marriage that was filled with constant unrest and turmoil, may believe that God "answered" their prayers when they entered into a new "perfect" peaceful marriage after a divorce even though this new marriage was invalid.

Whatever peace, satisfaction and joy such people find, cannot, in any way, come from God because they lack the grace necessary to possess the true peace found in union with Him.

Also, it must be remembered that there is such a thing as a peace which is nothing more than lack of worry that can be brought to a person by and through material situations. If, for example, a woman finally does leave a husband, who had caused her much trouble, with no intentions of remarrying, she may enter into a more peaceful way of life. However, this new-found freedom from daily tremors and explosions is not the peace I am talking about. It is only the result of a change in the person's daily life. As I said, even great sinners can find this type of a material peace.

The peace I am talking about is one in which the soul and whole being of the person are completely plunged into it. Its warmth and indescribable sweetness can be felt at all times, even when crosses come within the daily life. One of the tests, to discover if you do or do not have this peace, is to find out if it is still there when your daily life becomes filled with burdens and material turmoil.

Also, this peace will completely take away all fears, doubts and confusion about God and His ways. For this peace is not a solitary spiritual condition. It is more a combination of virtue, goodness, love for God, charity, purity of heart and above all: complete trust, faith and hope in God as well as total love for His holy will.

Trust, faith and hope in God, as well as love for His holy will, are a must if the person is to be gifted with the peace which I am talking about. Lack of this peace means lack of trust, faith and hope in God and in His will for the person.

Understanding God is of utmost importance. Very often people, instead of trying to find out God's will for them, make up their own desires of what they want to do and believe; then they ask God to approve their will for themselves. The trouble with such self-made plans is that they never include the cross, very seldom include penance or sacrifice, and more often than not, revolve around the person's own wishes for personal comforts, pleasures and happiness.

Trust, faith and hope are needed when God's will for the person does not correspond or agree with man-made plans and human desires. When crosses become the prize for daily struggles instead of golden rings of pleasure, the person must have enough faith in God's love for him or her to know that this love still exists, enough trust in God to know that He will help carry the crosses, and enough hope to know that after the crucifixion there will come the resurrection. Very few people have such a deep, lasting trust, faith and hope. That is one reason why so few people possess the type of inner peace which I am explaining. They may imagine that they do have true trust, faith and hope; however, when storm clouds appear, they soon discover how weak and fragile their trust, faith and hope really are.

Many times, I have seen people leave the Catholic religion when certain crosses are placed upon their shoulders, even if they had been faithful to the Church's teachings and sacraments. For example: there are numerous Catholics who leave the sacraments by and through an invalid marriage. Other Catholics will stop going to Mass and give up the sacraments when a loved one dies.

True trust, faith and hope are expanded and purified within a deep love for God's holy will. One can be saddened by a heavy cross, but unless the cross is accepted, there can be no inner peace. Unless the person can still dearly love God and also feel His love for them, there can be no inner peace. Unless the person can separate the spiritual values of God from the material standards of the world, there can be no inner peace. Unless the person can still hope in God's promises of eternal joy when all material delights disappear, there can be no inner peace.

When a person, by his or her climb up THE LADDER OF PERFECTION to the heights of Holy Abandonment, experiences the joys of a pure, deep, lasting inner peace, that person has a solid grip upon a life filled with unbelievable happiness no matter what daily crosses and problems he or she finds along the way that must be traveled.

Remember that a journey toward the fruits and rewards of Holy Abandonment is a quest for a lasting, pure, inner peace and happiness. Once this goal is reached, this peace and happiness will be eternal.

PART THREE

THE LIVING DESERT

INTRODUCTION

The term, The Living Desert, may not be familiar to everyone who seeks a more advanced prayer life; but it is my way of describing the highest form of the prayer stages which goes beyond and above the prayer of Holy Abandonment. Perhaps there is another name for this state of prayer; however, I chose the name, The Living Desert, for the following reason.

I, one day, read what a person had written in her spiritual diary. It appeared that this person had entered a realm of the prayer life which went beyond the prayer of Holy Abandonment. That, to me, was proof that one need not stop at the prayer of Holy Abandonment because there are always new heights to reach in a person's union with God; heights given to souls through the channels of grace.

As described by the woman in her personal writings, the name, The Living Desert, seemed to be most appropriate for this prayer stage. It seemed to consist of two important aspects of a desert; namely, silence and barrenness or emptiness.

The term, The Desert, is often used in spiritual books to describe a person's descent into The Dark Night Of The Soul; but I added the word living: The Living Desert. Because my desert is alive with pure sunlight, joy and peace which can only be experienced in the surroundings of the silence and emptiness found in a desert.

Allow me to present to my readers, the very words from that woman's diary which inspired me to write these chapters which tell of a most remarkable state of the prayer life which I call The Living Desert. These words were written in 1985:

I have experienced a most profound spiritual experience. One day, at Mass, it suddenly seemed to me that I was in a huge, empty space, almost like a desert, with no one and nothing there—except Christ. I had the most marvelous feeling that Christ and I were completely alone, in the sense that there were absolutely no barriers which prevented my total union with Christ. It seemed to me that this was my own soul completely devoid of all self-love or desires for material things which act as barriers to a pure union with Christ. All barriers were gone. Christ could come into this area for there was plenty of room for Him. Nothing was in the way of our holy union. And in this desert there existed such peace and calm, such joy and sweetness that I dared not even breathe within its confines for fear of disturbing this silence and wondrous peace brought by the presence of Christ. My spiritual director asked me what was the last barrier to fall. I replied: "It was not so much having barriers fall, as it was to reach a goal, a fulfillment of what I have sought. No more struggles or even distractions. Only pure, love peace, joy and happiness."

That is The Living Desert which I shall explain in the following chapters of this book.

L.D.

Chapter 1

THE LIVING DESERT

There is a stage or final development of union with God which goes beyond and above the prayer of Holy Abandonment. I call this stage The Living Desert. This development of the prayer life is far more intense and reaches far greater heights than all other types of prayer.

So sublime and majestic is this state or stage of spiritual development that I almost do not want to attempt to describe it. No earthly words can convey to the mind its exquisite spiritual beauty and joy. The fact is, I am almost afraid to bring before others this precious secret of the spiritual life for fear that people, not in tune with true spirituality and union with God, will completely misunderstand it and imagine that they have reached this state when in reality they are very far from it.

So the words which I now write must be seen by others as only a very rare glimpse or a very brief view into this exalted spiritual state and not a state which the average person could hope to enter. However, just knowing that such a stage or state does exist can bring tremendous joy, hope and encouragement to souls who have safely weathered many storms as he or she climbed THE LADDER OF PERFECTION to a certain place or state of union with God.

The soul can continue the climb knowing that there are always new heights to reach, new spiritual experiences to become involved in, new delights to share with God and new gifts of celestial endowments which one might be blessed with. In other words, when a person imagines that he or she has reached the top of THE LADDER OF PERFECTION, that person can become aware of the fact that, in reality, his or her climb has just begun.

There remains so much more to know and to experience.

The first thing to learn about this Desert state is that it is reserved for only the few souls God wishes to draw into it. It is impossible for any soul to enter this Desert by his or her own efforts or desires. Only God can carry the soul into that exalted state of union with Him; and this He does to very, very few souls. The reason for that is simple. Most souls never acquire the abundance of grace needed to partake of and understand such a union with God. As with all workings of the soul and spiritual life, grace and the given amount of grace within the soul determines the closeness of union with God. The higher one climbs THE LADDER, the more grace is required so that the person can experience and understand a closer union with Christ.

Much grace is abused or ignored by faint-hearted persons who become filled with doubts, fears and questions about God's holy will. The average person may rise to a very high level of sanctity and yet still abuse and ignore great amounts of grace which could be his or hers and, in that way, stop any further advancement. Most people will stop their own spiritual advancement by relying only upon their own efforts instead of allowing grace to lead them into a higher union with God. That is why a person who may appear to be a "living saint" may be on a very low level of union with God simply because he or she never acquired the added grace needed to advance to a higher state or stage. A person to whom God grants the blessings of entering into The Living Desert must allow grace to work its spiritual wonders without one ounce of resistance. That is a most difficult thing to do. There is always the human element which usually prevents a person from taking that final plunge into the total confidence and trust in God needed to acquire a very high union with Him. Even the ones who may at first respond to a direct call from God to enter into a closer union with Him, may suddenly hesitate and become filled with fear as the person sees his own spiritual limitations instead of what grace can do in spite of human weaknesses. A good example of that is when Christ called Peter to walk upon the waters. In a burst of joy-filled, pure confidence in Christ and His presence, Peter got out of the boat and did walk upon the waters.

But suddenly, Peter removed his eyes from Christ and saw himself and his human situation and limitations. When he did that, he quickly started to sink as fear took control of him. Such a Christ-Peter situation happens numerous times when grace is ignored and cast aside as human weaknesses rise to bring fears, doubts and confusion into the relationship.

When one considers The Living Desert state one must first of all know that to enter therein there must be a perfect, complete, unblemished total confidence, trust and faith in God developed by and through enormous amounts of grace received and used.

It is this grace which not only prepares the soul to enter into the Desert state, but it is also this grace which gives the understanding to the soul so that the person can fully comprehend what he or she is experiencing. So you can see how much grace is needed to understand and find the magnificent joys and spiritual delights found in this high union with God. You can also understand how useless it would be for God to draw a soul into such a state when the soul has not been prepared and purified by grace to enter therein.

This final infusion of grace and the receiving of this grace into the soul to prepare it for being transported into the Living Desert state is, as I have said, not given to many. The fact is, it is so rare to receive this grace that most saints never experienced this Living Desert state. That does not mean that a saint is less a saint because he or she did not experience this type of union with God. This state is not needed nor necessary for a person to become a saint. It is a pure gift of love to certain souls, and a very rare gift at that.

It occurs when God becomes so anxious for a soul to actually share some of the greatest delights of Heaven that He cannot wait for the person's actual death. So, it could be said, God brings Heaven to the soul.

The Living Desert state is, indeed, the closest union with God and the delights of Heaven which a person can experience on earth. This prayer state is truly the one wherein the soul can say: "It is not I who live, but Christ who lives in me and He had drawn me upward to taste the heavenly delights reserved for a soul in Heaven."

Chapter 2

PREPARATION FOR THE LIVING DESERT STATE

If a person is to be called into The Living Desert state of union with God, there cannot be a simple and sudden transfer from another stage or state into this final union. There has to be years of preparation and purification. So you can understand that someone just beginning to expand his prayer life cannot suddenly find himself transported into The Living Desert.

I personally knew of several people who imagined that they were right on top of THE LADDER OF PERFECTION in this Desert state when in reality they had not even built the platform upon which THE LADDER rests.

While it is possible for a soul to suddenly experience an overpowering feeling of the presence of Christ or an overwhelming love for Him, that experience is not entering the highest form, The Living Desert, of union with God. One reason being that the transfer into this Desert is not overpowering in such a way as to grab the senses and dramatically plunge the soul into this prayer stage.

What, in reality, happens is that the soul, after years of struggling, searching and suffering all sorts of torments and spiritual battles, finally finds the perfect place of total rest and peace. When the soul is allowed to enter this Desert, there is a tremendous peace which gently enfolds it. There is a silence so profound that the person does not dare breathe for fear of disturbing that peace and silence. There is a feeling that the soul has at last found its home after years of wandering upon stormy waters. It is a safe harbor where the soul feels completely free of all earthly cares and temptations. It is truly Heaven on earth where the soul and

Christ are as one: one thought, one joy, one peace, one love. This state of the prayer life is so precious that one dares not mention it for fear that the deepest secrets of one's union with God will be revealed to those not able to comprehend the wonder of it all or for fear that this Desert silence would be disturbed by probing inquiries.

However, as much as the soul fears that the silence of The Living Desert will be disturbed or even disappear, that cannot happen. Once the soul has been drawn into The Desert that exquisite spiritual experience will last forever. For that stage is the very threshold of eternity. The next and only step that the soul can then take is to cross that threshold and enter Heaven. That is one reason why the soul cannot enter this union on its own merits or desires. It is God alone who judges the sanctity of the person and calls the soul into The Living Desert. Only He knows when the proper purification and preparation for this Desert has been accomplished within the soul. The soul cannot see what God sees and knows because by the time the soul is ready to enter this union with God, the person has polished the precious virtue of humility to such a luster that if the person were asked if she were ready for The Living Desert, the person would automatically say no. Because of that, when the soul is lead by God into The Desert, the soul reacts with great amazement and wonderment never dreaming that such a spiritual treasure would be given to it; and at the same time knowing that never, not in one million years, will the soul leave such a blessed state of union with God.

But how is a soul prepared to enter such a union? The preparation takes place during the person's climb up THE LADDER to a closer union with God. The purification is accomplished by long years of struggle, spiritual battles, crosses, sufferings and prayers. There is no other way, not even by a powerful, mystical experience. The reason being that mystical experiences do not purify a soul, but only lead the soul's purification by producing a desire for a closer union with God.

However, 99 percent of the time, even after long years of struggle, sufferings and prayer, the soul is not allowed or called by God in this final union. The preparation and purification were never completed due to the person's own resistance to grace, misuse of grace or unwillingness to allow God to mold the soul as He so desires. The person, himself or herself builds barriers which are never removed. There are still traces of self-love, pride, lack of trust and so forth holding the soul back. The flexibility needed by God to mold the soul into what He desires the soul to be is never present. You can well imagine that only the most saintly people who practice heroic virtue can be called into The Living Desert stage, and there are few such people.

However, if one is called into The Living Desert what happens there? What does the soul experience? How does the soul know the difference between other states of union with God and this final state? I will answer such questions in the following chapters.

Chapter 3

DEVELOPING SIGNS

As a person's spiritual life develops, through the acceptance and use of grace, the soul experiences many profound changes as it continues its journey towards a more complete, a more perfect union with God. As each new and deeper prayer state or stage is entered, the soul feels and knows what new treasures it has gathered unto itself. There can be comparisons made between such things as the increase of inner joy and peace as new and different spiritual delights are given to the soul. A person comes to realize that these new experiences are ones he or she never had before. The person can also see and compare the difference between living with a variety of faults and human weaknesses and possessing virtues which he or she never had before.

In other words, the person can see and become aware of a great improvement in his or her personal relationship with God, with one's own inner way of life, as well as relationships to the situations and people in his daily life. When one reaches such heights as to be ready for The Living Desert, the acquisition of spiritual treasures has changed not only the spiritual life, but the material life as well.

That has to be. There can be no pretending or false illusions about these clear, noticeable differences. They are there and the person knows it. If there exists doubts, fears or uncertainties about whether or not these differences or changes have taken place, then the person has not entered the stage of union with God which he or she thinks has been entered.

Why are such differences and changes so unmistakenly vivid? Because, as the power of grace transforms the soul into the perfection of its union with the God who dwells deep within the soul, these same graces reflect upon material situations and human weaknesses destroying what barriers these bring to a person's complete union with God. In other words, the spiritual advancement cannot take place while such barriers remain. Only when these barriers are destroyed, can the soul advance to greater heights of union with God. As long as the barriers remain, there simply is no advancement. That is especially true when a soul is being prepared to enter The Desert state of union with God because within The Living Desert itself there are no barriers.

Now, as clear and vivid as the differences and changes are which the person can clearly see and notice, there is one change which is impossible to see and know. That is the next step upward towards union with God. A person can stand still, so to say, and look back and compare present spiritual experiences and improvements with past weakness, faults, etc.; however, the person cannot look ahead and imagine what spiritual experiences will be like in the future. Because of that, it is all too easy to assume that one has reached the top of THE LADDER OF PER-FECTION when in reality one may only be beginning the climb. Very often a deep, touching spiritual experience will be so overwhelming that the person will assume that nothing else exists beyond and above that one experience. But the truth of the matter is that the climb up that LADDER is never really finished until the person enters the very gates of Heaven. There are always new, wondrous spiritual experiences to be had which far outshine past or present ones.

If a person has the joys of entering The Living Desert, that person will know that the wondrous sweetness and joys found in that prayer stage are far greater than any experiences before. And if I had never explained about this Desert state, most people would never know it existed, because this state is well-hidden from human eyes and knowledge behind thick barriers build by human imperfections and weaknesses.

Even a person who has reached a very high degree of sanctity cannot imagine that there is a higher degree called The Living Desert. Yet, as the same time, such a person may experience spiritual enlightenments which could lead the soul into The Living Desert without realizing where such enlightenments are leading it. In other words, no one can understand or experience this Desert state until he or she has actually entered therein; however, there may very well be signs that the soul is being prepared to be drawn by God into The Living Desert.

The person may be given a very special grace or spiritual experience which had never been received by the soul before. The person may feel that "something" is about to happen deep within the soul, but has no idea what that "something" is. However, at this point, the soul begins to allow God more freedom with it. The soul becomes like clay, totally allowing the Divine Master to shape and mold it only as He desires. This becomes one of the signs that the soul may be allowed to enter The Living Desert, for no one can enter The Desert unless he or she completely allows God to mold and shape the soul as He so desires. There must be no resistance whatsoever. There must be a total, complete abandonment to God's holy will and a total, complete trust in that holy will. No more can such a person, in any way, try to manipulate God in an attempt to bring about personal desires or wishes. The choice to draw a soul into The Living Desert must be entirely God's; and the soul must give God the freedom He needs so as to draw the soul into The Living Desert.

Chapter 4

THE TURNING POINT

Although the preparation needed for a soul to be drawn into The Living Desert may take years and involve numerous spiritual battles, that one step into The Desert may come suddenly. One moment, the soul may be upon the battlefields and the next next moment it may enter into the silence and calm of The Living Desert. Then the person can look back and see what I call "The Turning Point." There has to be a turning point which is used by God to complete the soul's preparation for The Desert. It usually is a very special grace received by the soul which the person knows by its very nature that that one grace or blessing is far different than all others the soul has ever received. The person's soul is not yet in The Desert. The fact is, the person does not even, as yet, know that The Desert exists, but the person becomes aware of a new, different and more precious union with God complete with a knowledge of the fact that such a union the person never had before.

For example, the person may read a passage in the Bible such as: ". . .in heaven we shall be like God, for we shall see Him as he is" (*1 John* 3:2); and suddenly the soul will explode outward into a more complete, more perfect union with God. The person may actually experience the immense love, forgiveness and mercy of God which had never been experienced before. The person may feel that past sins, faults and weaknesses had completely vanished within the fire of divine love. The person may actually feel that he or she has entered into the bliss of Heaven, and the "return" to earth becomes most painful.

Although spiritual experiences may have happened before, this

Turning Point experience is far different because it is *lasting*! It does not fade away as do most spiritual experiences. It actually changes the person's whole outlook and attitude towards life and living. This type of a Turning Point experience is so profound, so intense that the person knows a most marvelous grace has been given to the soul, but as yet, does not know why. Then from that moment of The Turning Point to the actual entrance into The Living Desert, the person lives more in Heaven than on earth. It is at this point when God can carry the soul into The Desert. Before The Turning Point, that could not be possible.

Such a spiritual way of life is by no means becoming a fanatic. I always warn people about becoming a religious fanatic. There is a great deal of difference between a genuine purification of the soul and the enthusiasm of the fanatic. There can be noticed the purity of religion of the one whom God is preparing to enter into The Desert. Also the difference is the calmness, silence and humility of the one about to enter The Desert compared to the loud noise, activity and pride of the fanatic.

As I said The Turning Point spiritual experience is a lasting one. Many of the unimportant things in a person's life, which were once considered to be so important, are no longer of interest to the person. The person begins a life which is totally "Christ-centered." To the person, Christ is ever present, ever watching, ever loving. Many material situations, which used to bother and upset the person, no longer do. There is a tremendous calm in the spiritual as well as material life of the person because he or she feels so safe, so secure in God's love. A person could very well write such words as these: "Now there is a new stage of awareness of Christ's presence. It is a visible-invisible state of seeing Christ always before me, listening to all I say, watching all I do. It is the fulfillment of the statement: 'God sees all, God knows all.' I am no longer hidden in my human nature. Instead, I am in the state of complete exposure to Christ. . .the Christ who lives deep within my soul."

In addition, there is a tremendous desire for Heaven: to reach that final step on top of THE LADDER OF PERFECTION. So warmed by the fire of divine love is the soul that all attachments and love for material things fade away because nothing on earth could bring the warmth now felt by the soul being bathed in the pure love of God.

The person continues to faithfully fulfill all the duties and obligations of his or her daily life; however, there is now no strain or stress in doing such; because all is done for God with a tremendous love for God's holy will ever present. Life may still hold many crosses to be given to the person, but these crosses now reflect the brilliant light of the cross of Christ. In a word, The Turning Point experience is reflected in all the person does, says or thinks because the soul has been plunged into the all-embracing fire of divine love.

However, the soul still might not be drawn into The Desert. God may not desire or grant any other grace for the soul. That is why, even with a Turning Point experience, the person still does not know that The Living Desert exists. What the person is experiencing is so magnificent, so all-consuming that it does not seem possible that an even higher union with God is possible. It is only after the soul has been allowed to enter The Living Desert, only then can the person look back and see The Turning Point.

Chapter 5

PURE FAITH AND CONFIDENCE

Pure, unrestricted faith and confidence in God and in His holy will! What a blessing these two virtues are! But these blessings have a high price to be paid. These two virtues are among the very last to be acquired by anyone attempting to climb THE LADDER OF PERFECTION to a closer union with Christ. There are few, very, very, few people who have enough faith, trust and confidence in God, His grace, His love and His holy will to allow Him to mold their souls as He so desires.

Between the two extreme barriers, the people who figure they can mold their own souls without the help of God and His grace and the ones who tell themselves they are too unworthy to receive God's graces, there exist numerous barriers which people place between their souls and Christ who dwells within their souls.

The main purpose of the struggles up THE LADDER OF PER-FECTION is to destroy the barriers which prevent Christ from being clearly seen. The barriers which cause the most problems are lack of the faith, trust and confidence needed to reach a closer union with God.

Oh, it is so difficult to give up one's own will and desires! As one woman said to me one day: "Every day I get up and tell God how to run the world. . .but He never listens to me."

In much the same way most people tell God what they want from Him and what they do not want. When they get what they want, they praise and thank God. When they get what they don't want or not get what they want, they blame God, complain and go into various degrees of depression or anger. All the while, such barriers hinder or even destroy the person's union with Christ.

Many times a day most people will ask God: "Why?" Why did this happen to me? Why do all the "bad" people have all the good things in life? Why don't you answer my prayer? Why don't you hear me? Why do I have to suffer so when others never suffer? Etc. Etc.

No one, who has a "why" in his or her spiritual life used in the manner of objecting to or questioning God's holy will for that person, can enter into The Living Desert.

Each and every why, objection, or questioning of God's holy will acts as a barrier to the person's union with God. Each and every attempt to run away from, refuse to see, refuse to accept, or attempt to change God's will becomes a barrier which prevents a closer union with God.

Even when a person sinks into the state of what he or she thinks is humility and tells God that he or she is such a sinner that God's graces and blessings are not for him or her, that type of humility becomes a barrier which prevents the person's entry into The Desert.

The confidence, trust and faith in God and His will required to be called into The Desert is the most purest type. This type, of necessity, can only be acquired after years of struggling up THE LADDER. This type can only manifest itself after the person has destroyed all his or her barriers of why, objecting to, and questioning of God's holy will. And that is not an easy thing to do, not even for someone who may have reached a high degree of union with God.

As all the struggles went on as the person climbed THE LADDER OF PERFECTION, many large and small barriers fell within the person's spiritual life. Yet, there remained the barriers of doubts and fears which come when a person is not completely willing to surrender his or her will to God's.

It is only when the doubts and the fears turn into the total loving acceptance of God's holy will that the soul is prepared to enter into The Living Desert. It is only when the person completely surrenders his or her own will and desires to God, totally abandoning his or her own ideas and thoughts that the last barriers of lack of complete trust and faith in God's holy will disappear.

Let me give you examples of what I mean. Someone may be on a high level of union with God, yet the person may still be filled with fear thinking that he may not get to Heaven or may have to spend a long time in Purgatory. Another person may consider herself to be a very unhappy person and decides that if only what she really wants happens that is the only way she can be happy. Another person may still wonder if God loves him even though he has personally experienced many signs of God's love for him. Someone else may truly love God, His holy will. The person may be most faithful to daily prayer and Mass attendance until a loved one dies suddenly. Then the person wants to "punish" God for this cross by no longer going to Mass or praying. I could go on and on with stories of where and when someone's own desires and will conflict with God's.

People constantly want to manipulate God, to tune Him in to what they want, to control His will for them.

This very serious spiritual fault can be found in people who may be considered by many to be living saints as well as in great sinners. All the attempts to manipulate God, to refuse to see His will, to refuse to accept His will, to try to have Him change His ways instead of having the person change his or her ways become a sign of the person's lack of trust, faith and confidence in God's holy will for them.

Now compare these examples with the type of trust, confidence and faith which is needed by someone who may be called into The Living Desert.

This pure, holy confidence, trust and faith is expressed when the person reaches the point in his or her spiritual life when the person does not have one ounce of fear or doubts about what life may hold.

Do not confuse this with a person's indifference towards life and living which could be a mental illness. There are no disorders in the type of confidence, trust and faith I am talking about. There is only a beautiful inner peace found by the person who knows without any doubts or fears that God knows what is best for the person and his or her life.

There is a supernatural joy deep within the person as he lovingly and completely abandons his will and life to God. There is a wondrous emptiness of one's own self-love, self-desires, self-wants. There is an instant giving up of ways or bad habits which may interfere with God's will in any way. There is the pure faith, trust and confidence to be able to say to God, even with tears in the person's eyes: "That is all right, dearest Lord, I don't mind. I so love and accept your holy will. Your will is my will."

When a person has finally reached this point in his or her spiritual life, God can come forth to mold the person's soul as He wants because the person has unmolded the type of soul he or she imagines the soul should be. Then the person is ready to be called into The Living Desert.

Chapter 6

THE ENTRANCE INTO THE LIVING DESERT

Now God calls the soul into The Living Desert. How does a person know this has happened? What can one expect to find in The Living Desert? Why is this prayer stage far different from all others?

When a person actually enters into The Living Desert state of union with God, many profound changes occur within the person's material and spiritual life.

The very first spiritual change the soul experiences in The Desert is to suddenly notice the absence of spiritual turmoil and conflicts. Up to that point, the soul has spent years struggling up THE LADDER OF PERFECTION daily, even hourly, fighting spiritual battles. The soul knows well the conflicts, torments, spiritual darkness and suffering found upon these battlefields. Very often, there were even inner struggles and battles whenever the person wanted to do a good deed or pray, etc.

The soul is so used to being upon these battlefields that the very first thing it notices after entering The Desert is the disappearance of all spiritual struggles and conflicts.

The soul looks around unable to believe that such calmness and peace actually exists; not only when the person prays, but also throughout the day no matter where the person goes or what duties and responsibilities are fulfilled. Being in The Desert is not just for prayer time, but it becomes a way of life. The soul has never before experienced such tranquility. So profound is this experience that the person does not even want to breathe for fear that a simple breath would disturb the all-consuming peace and quietness of The Desert stage.

The person feels it has entered a strange, new world; one which the soul never even knew existed. The soul waits, prepared for another spiritual battle or conflict as it has done for years— but nothing happens. There is only this perfect peace and calmness. That is one reason why The Desert stage can only come at the end or top of THE LADDER. Unless and until the soul has gone through all sorts of spiritual battles and struggles, the soul could never know the difference between these struggles and battles and the non-struggles of The Living Desert state.

Then the soul discovers, much to its amazement and joy, that all struggles have vanished in regards to prayer. Even in the higher stages of prayer, often there remains little struggles, such as the person still being tempted not to pray or not to go to Mass or using the time allotted for prayer for something else. But once the soul has been called into The Living Desert all such temptations and struggles simply vanish. The soul plunges itself into the wondrous, refreshing waters of prayer without one *ounce* of *resistance* completely enjoying prayer in a way the soul never experienced before. The person can, at any given moment, any time of the day or night close his or her eyes and instantly enter into all sorts of prayer: vocal prayer, mental prayer, meditation and, of course, the higher stages of contemplation. All that is done without one ounce of struggle or resistance.

At last the soul finds the freedom to pray exactly as it always wanted to pray without any interference. At last the soul finds the pure joys of prayer where not one ounce of former problems exist. The person begins to wonder why such problems ever existed in the first place. The person will ask herself: "But it is so easy to pray. Why did I find it such a struggle just to get down to the business of praying?" The person becomes a bit confused wondering why there had been any problems in the prayer life when, in reality, prayer is so easy, so simple. The person will actually forget all the struggles that had been found in developing a prayer life; so much so, that the person may wonder why prayer is so difficult for others when it is "so simple, so easy" to pray. The person will say: "Pray often. It is so easy to turn one's mind to God and to prayer," not realizing that he or she has entered a level of the prayer life which few people enter or experience. The virtue of humility keeps the person from realizing that he or she has been given extraordinary graces which others do not possess.

As the person experiences more and different treasures found in The Living Desert, the person may even be puzzled by the fact that others, on a low level of spirituality, find so many spiritual problems and barriers. Once again, the profound humility which of necessity has to be within the person's soul in order to enter into The Living Desert, causes the person to fail to realize that his or her own spiritual advancement far outshines that of those just starting their spiritual journey to a closer union with God.

Chapter 7

THE SILENCE AND EMPTINESS OF
THE LIVING DESERT

Once the person is called into The Living Desert, the first and most profound lasting impression the person has is to be drawn into an indescribable calmness and silence. This calmness and silence is so overpowering that the person does not want to even breathe for fear that a single breath taken would disturb the calmness and silence.

It is this experience of silence and calmness which tells the person that he or she has been drawn into a new and different stage of prayer and union with Christ, one the person did not even know existed.

Along with the intense feelings of the calmness and silence of The Living Desert, there is a most unique spiritual sensation of the emptiness of The Desert.

The soul looks all around and far into the distance and sees nothing: total complete emptiness. This has never happened before.

All throughout the torturous struggle to reach a closer union with Christ, there had been much turmoil, even agony, deep within the soul. There had also been numerous barriers crowded into the confines of a person's spiritual life. Even within the higher stages or states of prayer, such as contemplation, some inner struggles and some pesky, annoying barriers still remain. Not so when one enters the Living Desert.

I am not saying that all barriers, such as minor faults and human weaknesses, disappear for they remain until death. What I am saying is that all barriers, which hindered a person's complete union with Christ, disappear.

As the soul looks around and far into the distance, the soul sees nothing: nothing, except Christ. The Christ, whom the soul had so faithfully struggled for so long to find is now completely visible with nothing to block the view. The soul and Christ with no barriers to block the soul's view of Christ, that is the highest prayer state the soul can reach, that is The Living Desert.

Then the person is no longer hidden in his or her human nature. The person not only has Christ completely in view, but the person's soul is in a state of complete exposure to Christ as He stands so clearly before the eyes of the soul. Then there suddenly exists a wondrous harmony of wills, of love, of joy and of peace. Truly it is not the person who lives, but Christ in the person who is now in control of the person's whole being. The person has finally allowed Christ to mold his or her soul as Christ so desired. The soul is now ready, not only to have a most complete union with Christ, but also to no longer resist God's will. The person now allows God to give to the soul His choicest blessings and graces without one ounce of resistance. And this is what God wanted to do throughout all the years of the person's struggled to climb THE LADDER OF PERFECTION: to give to the soul His choicest graces and blessings.

The soul stands empty of all love for material things, self-love, spiritual problems and barriers and becomes as a barren desert ready to be filled with God's choicest blessings and graces.

Then the soul learns completely the truth that the soul always wins, the soul never loses as it struggles towards perfection. For what really happens in this struggle is that God is only waiting for the opportunities to give choice blessings and graces to the soul. In other words, He asks nothing from the person except the opportunities to lavish His spiritual treasures upon the soul and mold the soul as He so desires.

And how long a wait it is! There are few, very few souls who honestly and completely believe that God desires only the opportunities to enrich the soul and, in that way, to draw the soul into a closer union with Him if only the person would accept and use His grace to destroy all barriers that prevent a closer union with Him.

Chapter 8

MORE INSIGHTS INTO THE LIVING DESERT

When a person has the unique privilege of being called into The Living Desert, it does not take long for the person to become aware that something wondrous has been given to him or her. At first, the person may be confused by the situation, but this confusion quickly disappears as the brilliant light of Christ's nearness bathes the soul in waves of refreshment, peace and joy which do not cease.

At first when the soul is allowed into The Living Desert, it seems as if The Desert surrounds the person completely engulfing the soul. But then other wondrous, overpowering insights are given to the soul.

The soul discovers that The Living Desert has become a sort of spiritual barrier in itself, but this time it prevents human ideas, thoughts, emotions and all sorts of distractions from reaching the inner depths of the person's being wherein exists only perfect peace, joy and happiness brought to the soul by the clear view of Christ.

As the spiritual experience deepens, the person discovers that many faults and human weaknesses embedded in human nature, and the effects of such, cannot reach the person's inner being nor disturb the soul's relationship with Christ.

For example: if someone does something one doesn't like or says something one doesn't like, it is only natural for the person to see the "bad" of it all and express complaints or even uncharitable words. Also, it is only natural for a person to worry about something or to fear something or to get annoyed with someone and have thoughts build up from a "mole" to a "mountain" over

177

a little, unimportant incident.

The soul soon discovers that these perfectly human faults and weaknesses are prevented from reaching the inner desert the soul now exists in. Also, the person has the insight to compare the human with the divine, and soon realizes that the desert stage or state of the prayer life has to be the nearest thing to experiencing the delights of Heaven that is possible for a human being on earth to so experience. The person actually is given the knowledge and the feelings of the purity of Heaven wherein even the smallest fault or human weakness can vanish forever in the fire of pure love.

That does not mean that all human faults and weaknesses disappear. (There were many faults and weaknesses found in the saints.) What it means is that the soul experiences the total absence of the effects or results of such faults and weaknesses deep within The Desert state of the soul.

Compare that to the turmoil, anxiety, self-blaming and suffering even a tiny fault can cause someone in a lower state of union with God.

What the soul experiences is that while living a human life complete with all human problems, crosses, faults and weaknesses, the soul also experiences the state of a human soul in Heaven.

Another remarkable insight which is given to the soul is the following: While the person had been well aware of his or her sins, faults and weaknesses as the climb up THE LADDER continued, The Desert surprises the person by revealing a few faults the person never knew existed. The soul becomes aware that there is yet a purification still needed; however, this purification is to be done solely by and through God's infinite love. In other words, the soul cannot feel the effects of these hidden faults because they quickly disappear in the brilliant flames of God's love as paper would disappear in the flames of a roaring fire. In that case, there is no need for worry, fear or anxiety when such faults are revealed because they disappear as quickly as they are revealed.

No longer are spiritual battles, inner torments, great sufferings, etc. needed for these final stages of purification. The gentle touch of God's love is all that is needed. God treats the soul like a fragile infant so tenderly, so lovingly because He does not wish to disturb the rare, priceless flower He has fashioned by and through His grace and love.

The divine artist previously had chiseled, cut and shaped the soul through periods of darkness, pain, torment and sufferings. But now that the magnificent work of art is in full bloom, now only a master artist's final touches are needed.

The divine artist carefully and, oh, so gently, places the final adornments upon His masterpiece. All is done in love, peace and joy; and the soul at last fully understands the infinite peace, joy and love of God.

The soul can then look at God as if the soul looks into a mirror and see itself as God sees it: a precious work of art which the soul allowed God to fashion with His grace and love as He so desired.

If people could only realize that truth! If people could only allow God to fashion and mold their souls, what wondrous works of art He could produce! But the person resists a "million" times as the person clings to his or her own ideas, sins, desires, wants and so forth. The human pride which can infiltrate even noble desires for holiness prevents the divine artist from accomplishing the work of art He so longs to create.

Chapter 9

THE DESERT'S ACCESSIBILITY

One of the most amazing insights given to the person whose soul has entered The Living Desert is the following.

The person soon discovers that nothing can take him or her out of The Living Desert.

The person can freely fulfill all the duties and obligations of life. The person can be involved with and become burdened with all sorts of crosses and problems. The person can deal with all types of people, and their problems; and yet, the person can at any given moment of the day or night simply close his or her eyes or raise his or her heart to God and instantly the person finds The Desert.

One of the most frustrating aspects of the spiritual life is when a person has a magnificent feeling of God's presence and love, and then the feeling quickly vanishes.

The person will begin a search to recapture that moment. Some people will search "the world over" trying to find what was lost. Often such a search goes on for years, sometimes a lifetime.

I once met a woman who had had such a spiritual experience and who lost the feeling. She told me she went all over the world to all the famous Shrines to try and find what she had lost. She never found it.

Such a thing never happens to the person who has entered The Living Desert. Why? Because the person never leaves the Desert. The Desert surrounds the person. The person is always in the middle of it.

In other words, the person now lives a life centered around Christ, His love, His ways and His will; and the eyes of the soul never are taken away from Him. No matter in what direction the eyes of the soul look, Christ is clearly in view.

Another reason why The Living Desert is so accessible is because The Desert is free from all material distractions. Naturally a person's daily life presents countless distractions, problems, etc. Until the person enters The Desert, such distractions can severely affect the spiritual life. Often a person's spiritual advancement is stopped or curtailed by the problems or work of a daily life. Often it can be years before another step up THE LADDER OF PERFECTION can be taken. Just as often any advancement is counteracted by a material situation which could destroy the progress made or end any future progress. More often than not, a person, who sincerely wants to have a closer union with God, becomes frustrated when prayer time becomes merely a period of fighting one distraction after another. Not so when a person enters The Desert. Why?

For one reason, as I said, the person never leaves The Desert. Nor does the person lose the sight of Christ within The Desert.

By the time the person enters The Living Desert nothing can distract the person from Christ who dwells deep within the soul. Even a day filled with hectic activity cannot destroy the relationship the soul has with Christ who dwells deep within the soul. The person's inner being constantly feels the love and peace given to it by Christ. The person has only to raise the mind and heart to God, for a second, and the soul becomes bathed in the sweetness and joy of Christ's presence and love; so much so, that often the person wants to shout with joy. The person can say: "I can close my eyes in silence, and instantly God's pure love floods my whole being."

The fact is, the person may increase daily activity especially acts of charity, so filled with joy is he or she and so willing is the person to carry out God's will for him or her in the state of life God had willed.

It is very important for me to state that no one has to "go away" to some far distant "mission field" in order to serve God and to advance spiritually to the point when entrance into The Desert is a possibility. I have said often, and I will say it here: sanctity is as near as your parish church wherein you find the sacraments and the Mass. The Desert state of prayer proves that.

As the person carries out daily duties and obligations, the person's soul is constantly bathed in the warmth and light of The Desert. Nothing on earth can distract the soul from that light and warmth. The person, who has been allowed in The Desert finds, constantly, tremendous joy as this discovery is made. The person, who previously may have had prayer time plagued with distractions, finds the tremendous relief and joy of being able to spend long periods of time praying without any distractions, bathed in the warmth and light of Christ's nearness and love.

The person can also, at will, enter into any state or stage of the prayer life from vocal prayer to advance forms of contemplation.

The freedom of the soul to so interact with all forms of prayer is another constant, never-ending, joy-filled experience filled with amazement.

There were many times, during the spiritual growth of the person when certain types of prayer, such as mental prayer, had been so difficult that such prayers had to be abandoned for a time. But now, this same person can easily and freely go from vocal prayers, to mental prayers, to contemplation and experience tremendous joy in each stage of prayer.

The reason for that is the person constantly exists in a state of prayer. The Desert is a never-ending prayer. Although there are no outward signs that the person is praying other than when seen in church or saying the Rosary with others, etc., the person actually prays day and night without ceasing. How? By never losing sight of Christ. No matter where the eyes of the soul look, there is Christ, Christ to be loved by a mere glance or a sweet word.

Chapter 10

WALKING DEEPER INTO THE LIVING DESERT

Once the person has entered The Living Desert, he or she is there forever. There is no turning back. The Desert does not disappear. It is ever present, ever near, ever real. There can be no other beginnings for another or different type of spiritual journey. That is one reason why The Living Desert state of union with God has to be found only on top of THE LADDER or at the end of the quest for union with God.

In all other states or stages of union with God, there can be seen incomplete spiritual experiences. One starts to climb towards union with God and suddenly falls away or gives up or changes direction. An overpowering spiritual experience, such as might occur in sincere quests for perfection, will disappear or fade or demand an ever greater experience. First bursts of enthusiasm disappear often leaving the person in a state of depression. Spiritual struggles and temptations overwhelm the person causing many emotional problems to develop. A person may wonder: "How is it that yesterday I was so on fire with love for God and today the fire is gone. I feel nothing but emptiness. I cannot even pray. I feel God is gone and I am left with nothing."

Daily crosses and sufferings quickly cause the person to question God's will, to object to it, to refuse to accept it. Numerous examples can be found wherein a heavy cross placed upon shoulders, not willing to accept the cross, quickly destroyed the person's desire and quest for a closer union with God.

Often a person may think that he or she has indeed reached the "top" of THE LADDER only to discover how quickly one can fall when a strong temptation destroys good, holy intentions and desires. Then comes the excuses, the searchings for valid reasons why the fall occurred, the blaming of others, even God, the inability to acknowledge one's own weaknesses and even sins.

When one has truly entered into The Living Desert all such problems, conflicts and spiritual battles completely disappear. . .and I mean disappear. If such problems, conflicts and battles still remain, even a trace of them, the person simply has *not* entered The Living Desert.

That does not mean that all temptations, crosses and problems disappear. It means that the battles and inner conflicts caused by temptations, crosses and problems, disappear. In other words, in spite of the fact that daily life continues with all its problems, crosses and sufferings, these cannot disturb the wondrous peace and quietness found in The Desert. The person is completely free of all the usual spiritual battles and results of these conflicts which are caused by daily problems, crosses and sufferings. Why is that?

The reason why the person's Desert state remains ever calm and peaceful is that once The Living Desert has been entered, material and spiritual conflicts cannot enter.

One of the greatest spiritual treasures found in The Desert is the complete absence of barriers which prevent the fullness of the person's union with Christ. Within The Desert there exists only Christ and the soul. That is why I call it The Desert. The soul looks around, far and near, and finds *nothing except Christ*. Christ and the soul, alone in perfect joy, peace and pure love. There are no barriers, nothing to separate them, nothing to interfere with the divine communications between the soul and Christ.

When the soul enters The Desert, the soul immediately knows that a wondrous new spiritual experience has been allowed to happen. As the soul penetrates deeper into The Desert new and even more wondrous spiritual experiences are to be found. New and marvelous insights are given to the soul. The person, as I said, at first wonders why prayer is "so simple, so easy," why others find so many conflicts and spiritual battles, and so forth. But as the soul goes deeper into The Living Desert many insights are given to the person as the precious gifts of the Holy Spirit

Wisdom and Understanding become full, magnificent flowers; whereas before they were only tiny buds struggling to reveal all their heavenly beauty as flowers in full bloom.

Chapter 11

THE LIVING DESERT EXPANDS

Once the person has become used to The Living Desert (and it will take some time to experience all the different aspects of The Desert), once the person begins to enjoy all the freedom and spiritual delights of The Living Desert, new insights are given to the person.

The person's soul looks around at the vast emptiness of The Desert, completely void of any barriers, and discovers that as long as no material barriers exist in The Desert, there is a great deal of room for heavenly angels or saints. So the person discovers he or she has another freedom found only in The Desert. That is the freedom to call into The Desert whomever the person desires.

As I said, in the last chapter, The Desert state itself is a prayer. So, within this state of prayer, prayers to the Holy Mother of God, to saints or angels are most acceptable and suitable. So the person can call into The Desert, the Holy Mother of God by saying the Rosary or a given saint by saying prayers to that saint.

The person can also turn the whole desert into scenes from the Bible or from the life of Christ or Mary. When this happens, there is the immense joy of being able to meditate without distractions or interference. Thus, it is not unusual for a person who has entered The Living Desert to meditate upon all the mysteries of the Rosary at one time without any distractions. That is possible because there are no distractions in the Desert. The person can merely place the mental picture of the scene he or she wants to meditate upon and the scene remains clear until the person wants to change it into something else.

Needless to say, the prayer-conversations which the person has with Christ, Our Lady or a saint are completely meaningful and filled with pure love and joy. The intense silence of The Desert allows the person to speak clearly to whomever he or she desires to speak to. No longer does the person have to struggle among "a million" distracting thoughts to tell Christ or Our Lady or a saint what he or she wants to say.

The attention span of the person in The Desert is absolutely amazing. Some saints have been known to remain in this state of undivided attention to Christ or Our Lady for days at a time. Others have been known to be in an intense state of prayer even while faithfully fulfilling their daily duties and obligations. So cleverly is this done, that others around the saint may not even notice what is happening deep within the saint's soul.

Once again, such is possible because once the person enters The Desert, this desert never disappears. The person is in The Desert every moment of every day constantly feeling the warmth and inner peace of Christ's presence and love.

While the person can call into The Desert Our Lady or saints or angels or mental pictures, it must be clearly understood that these mental pictures are *not visions or apparitions*! The fact is, visions or apparitions are rare in The Desert stage. Although most people might believe that The Living Desert would be the "perfect" place for Christ or Our Lady to actually appear to the person, that is not true. Why? Because the soul is so in tune with God and His holy will, the soul is so surrounded by the love of God, the soul is so bathed in the light of God's presence that visions are not necessary.

If you were to think about it, you will see what I mean. Think about the visions to Bernadette at Lourdes or the children at Fatima. These children were definitely not in The Desert state of the prayer life, yet they saw visions. Visions of this kind can come to anyone, even to someone who may not, at the time of the vision, be considered to be holy or saintly. Visions are given for special, precise reasons and not as rewards to someone who has achieved a high degree of sanctity. And someone who never saw a vision can still acquire the holiness necessary to be called into The Desert.

That is because holiness comes from grace, the sacraments and the direct action of the Holy Spirit upon a soul, visions may not. Visions are not necessary for holiness or even for salvation: grace is. Visions can often confuse a person's spiritual life; being in The Desert cannot. And, even if a person does have visions as he or she climbs THE LADDER OF PERFECTION, the person must still purify his or her soul by and through the ordinary means of sanctification.

Also, the person can call into The Living Desert whomever he or she desires. Visions and other mystical experiences cannot be brought into reality through any act or desire of the person; although, false visionaries rather imagine they have such a power. A true vision is sent to the person who usually does not expect such a blessing nor desires it.

On the other hand, Mary's love and care for the person is very much alive and felt especially within The Desert state or stage of the prayer life. The person, who has been called into this magnificent prayer state, not only finds wondrous joys being with Christ, but also being with Mary. That is because Mary is always there right next to her beloved Son.

To turn one's attention to Mary (or to a saint) is, by no means, to turn away from Christ. When one has reached the point of always seeing Christ, with the eyes of the soul, one cannot help but see His beloved Mother. And that is a very beautiful experience because Mary is truly loved by all who have reached this high state of union with Christ, her Son.

Chapter 12

THE LIVING DESERT BLOOMS

Once the person is allowed into The Living Desert, the mystical favors received by the soul therein never cease. The Desert, in spite of its name, is not a barren wasteland. I call this prayer state The Desert because it is empty of all barriers and material distractions. Actually, The Desert is alive with extraordinary gifts for the soul. Also for the person there are beautiful flowers which never wither or die.

The very first precious flower found in The Desert is a magnificent joy which the soul becomes bathed in and which spreads outward into the person's daily life. It is true, that there never was a sad-faced saint. A pure, holy, lasting joy is one of the fruits found in the higher forms of union with God, especially contemplation. When one has entered The Desert, this joy increases. As waves of sweetness and peace constantly cover the soul, so also do waves of joy, in a never-ending surge.

This joy has to be explained for it is a far different joy than one normally has when, for example, the person receives a gift he is especially pleased with. This joy has to be understood in the context of from where the joy comes; namely, Christ. Christ shares His divine, infinite joy with the person. If He ever went out of view, then nothing on earth could cause the person the type of joy found in knowing that he or she lives in the presence of Christ and He is clearly in view. The joy comes from the fact that the person lives a Christ-centered life and not because the person has many material possessions.

That being the case, this joy never disappears no matter how many problems, crosses or sufferings the person has.

Very often someone, who is on his or her journey up THE LADDER OF PERFECTION, can have a fleeting taste of this joy. But a cross or problem can make it quickly disappear. Not so when one is in The Desert. The reason is clear. Christ never goes out of sight and the mere sight of Christ causes the soul to be bathed in pure joy.

This joy is not hidden deep within the person's soul. The person cannot hide it. So the person becomes a very joy-filled person—not expressing a wild burst of enthusiasm and joy as do some who are in prayer groups—but a most beautiful, peaceful, deep-felt type of joy. Others see the person as a very pleasant one who can give to them a taste of his or her own joy just by being near.

In addition, the person who has been allowed into The Desert finds other flowers and fruits which exist in this prayer state. The person, because he or she has found so great a peace and joy, turns outward towards others in an attempt to have others share these precious gifts. The person has a great deal of compassion and sympathy for others. The person is willing to help others, especially the ones who still are struggling to reach a closer union with God.

Other blooms are found in The Desert which reflect their light into the daily life of the person who has entered therein. The person will be able to hide most, if not all, of his or her personal crosses and problems and sufferings. The person can be very ill, yet no one will notice because of the joy and peace on the face and because of the person's attempts to help others in spite of his or her own crosses and sufferings.

The person can find much joy in his or her daily life instead of only complaining about everyone and everything.

More flowers bloom: the person can have a very deep understanding of God, His ways and the way God works with others and through others.

The person can always find the way God brings good out of even bad situations.

The person can express a trust and faith in God, which cause people to wonder, for they themselves have no such trust or faith.

In regards to innocent, material joys and pleasures, the person accepts these also as God's holy will and does not run away from them. But the person is most willing to share them with others. So the person who is in The Living Desert can see and accept God's many material blessings and find great enjoyment in such simple things as a walk in the park with a friend or a dinner in a restaurant with friends or families. However, there is a very thick shield which prevents any material joy from disturbing the peace and calmness of The Desert or distracting the eyes of the soul from Christ.

Daily, new flowers of grace are discovered by the person's soul as the soul wanders around The Desert ever watching Christ, ever walking in the light of His nearness.

By then, the soul and Christ are so one, so in tune, that never are there any distorted notes heard in the sweet, melodious songs sung between them.

But how can a person live a plain, normal daily life under such circumstances? The following chapters explain how that is done.

Chapter 13

THE LIVING DESERT AND DAILY LIFE

One of the insights given to the person who has the immense joys of being allowed into The Living Desert state of union with God, is to know how to use this state in daily life. That is very important to learn because, as I said, this state or stage is far different than any other of the prayer life because it also becomes a way of life as one fulfills daily duties and obligations.

The Desert, once entered into, always remains. It does not disappear. The person stays in this desert.

But, how can one still live a daily life of work, problems, joys, sorrows, crosses and sufferings? Does one "leave" daily life and live as if one were in some kind of a mystical trance completely unaware of what is happening all around and in that life? Does the person close his or her eyes and ears to the sounds of the world, to the plaintive cry of the human sufferings of mankind, to the evil, sin and corruption existing in the world or to the wondrous daily little "miracles" sent by a God who still cares for His children?

No, one does not. For if the person desires to "leave" ordinary daily life and the world in his or her state of life, then that person simply has not entered The Desert.

Why? Because when one has truly and completely entered into The Desert, the person does not leave his or her state of life (lay person or religious) because The Desert *comes* to the person. The person does not go into The Desert in the sense that he or she leaves the state of life God willed for the person. The Desert comes into that life.

And that is a marvelous thing to know. For centuries most lay people believed that only a religious, in a convent or monastery, could reach a high degree of union with God. They felt that the pressures and distractions of a life of a lay person prevented spiritual advancement to a closer union with God. The truth of the matter is that God's grace can touch a soul no matter what state of life the person is in and it is grace that brings about the wondrous spiritual gifts of union with God, not a running away from daily duties and responsibilities.

The fact is that the person who has entered into The Living Desert is fully aware of and quite capable of fulfilling daily duties and responsibilities. Remember that this Desert state comes only after long years of struggling up THE LADDER OF PERFECTION. By the time a person is permitted to enter into that stage, there can be no desires to change one's state of life. All the battles to reach such a high union with God have occurred in the state of life God willed for the person, be it lay or religious. That being the case, The Desert state does not remove the person from his or her daily duties and responsibilities.

However, it is possible that once a lay person's daily duties and responsibilities cease, such as children who grow up and leave home or the death of a spouse, the person will be free to change from the lay state into the religious one so that he or she can experience the spiritual delights found in a life of prayer and contemplation without the constant distractions of family or work-related problems and conflicts.

But such a change would be rare and really not necessary at all because The Desert state or stage of the prayer life brings such exquisite, inner spiritual joys and peace that whatever the soul longed and hungered for in its quest for a more complete union with God is completely fulfilled.

So, the transfer into The Living Desert is not at all disruptive in regards to daily life and living, problems, crosses or innocent enjoyments. Family, friends or work-related problems can continue, but they cannot disturb the soul's wondrous state of union with God.

Why is that? Because when the soul has entered The Living Desert, the person has acquired tremendous spiritual insight and wisdom to see the "nothingness" of earth and the "greatness" of Heaven. In other words, the person looks at life in a far different way than previously.

The main reason being, all the person's inner, spiritual conflicts have ceased. That is one of the gifts or rewards of being allowed into The Desert. When I say "ceased," that is exactly what I mean. Spiritual battles, some of which may have lasted for years, completely disappear. All doubts, fears, worries, spiritual struggles, dark nights of the soul, etc., disappear. As I said, if such struggles, doubts, etc. remain, then the person has not entered into The Desert.

The person no longer questions God's ways, the person no longer feels that God is "far away," the person no longer feels that God "doesn't hear" his or her prayers, the person no longer is bothered with overwhelming temptations.

In place of all such spiritual problems, barriers and conflicts, there is an unending, pure, delightful joy which constantly flows over the soul in warm, refreshing waves in much the same way as never-ending, moving waves of an ocean roll up upon the shore.

Prayer becomes filled with precious moments of intimate union with God as the brilliant light of His love illuminates the soul and dispels all darkness. Each moment of prayer becomes an always new, wondrous experience; so much so, that the prayer lingers, not just as a memory, but as a living, vibrating part of daily life.

With such an active spiritual life, daily problems and even conflicts cannot cause the concern, worry or discouragement that they once did. The soul always rises above them filled with hope and tremendous trust and faith in the mercy, the goodness, the love of a gentle, caring God. Daily duties and obligations become a joy, whereas they once seemed to be so burdensome. Why? Because the person has a tremendous love for God's holy will. When this love is put into practice, the person can readily accept daily life knowing that he or she is in the state of life wherein God wills the perfection and sanctification of the soul. And the person is so in tune with the ways of God that he or she can use all in a daily life for the good of the soul.

Such an attitude is clearly shown in a prayer such as the following one:

MORNING OFFERING

My Dearest Jesus, I offer to Your Sacred Heart through the Immaculate Heart of Mary all my prayers, works, good deeds, sufferings, sacrifices, penances and mortifications, whatever I do, whatever I say today. May everything I do, say and think be used only for the good of my soul and for the good of the souls of others.

I wish to gain all the merits, graces, blessings and indulgences I can gain this day especially from all the Masses said and all the communions received. May they all come to me, then go outward to help save souls and release the souls from Purgatory.

I wish to accept with much love for Your Holy Will, whatever crosses, sufferings and sorrows you care to send to me. May they all be used only for the good of my soul and the good of the souls of others. Amen.

Cum Permissu Superiorum
—John F. Whealon, D.D.
Archbishop of Hartford

Maryheart Crusaders 6/5/86

Chapter 14

THE LIVING DESERT AND
FAULTS AND WEAKNESSES

When a person actually enters The Living Desert, do all faults and human weaknesses disappear as if by magic? If not, then how does one cope with still having human faults and weaknesses when the person exists on such a high level of union with God?

First of all, as I said before, the entrance into The Desert does not remove the person from daily life and living. The opposite is true. So intense is the person's awareness of a Christ-centered life that the person wants to live daily life to the fullest so as to glorify and praise God within the daily duties and obligations which God has willed for the person in his or her state of life.

Fulfilling such duties and obligations become, for the person, a daily prayer of love for God. The person is so in tune with God's holy will that daily duties become just another way to say to God: "I do this, not because I have to but because I so love your holy will for me."

The person, who has reached such a high union with God, actually looks for ways in his or her daily life not only to fulfill God's holy will, but to reach out to others in acts of pure charity and love. So, such a person becomes a very active person (to the extent that personal health allows) always looking for opportunities to touch the lives of others with a very rare, and beautiful charity. In doing so, there are bound to be human misunderstandings, conflicts and disagreements simply because other people are not on the same spiritual level. Along with these misunderstandings and conflicts, human weaknesses and faults show clearly, including the faults and weaknesses of the person who has entered The Desert.

How does that person cope with these faults and weaknesses?

First of all, the faults and weaknesses are no surprise to the person. He or she is fully aware that these faults exist. The fact is, the whole climb up THE LADDER OF PERFECTION included daily battles to overcome human faults and weaknesses. The person has already had numerous spiritual battles trying to overcome human faults and weaknesses but still some remain. The fact is, the closer union a person acquires to the Christ who dwells deep within the soul, the more aware the person becomes of human faults and weaknesses within the confines of a human nature weakened by the fall of our first parents. If the person who has entered The Living Desert is told about his or her own faults, the person would readily agree that these faults do indeed exist; and the person would be most willing to say such a prayer as follows:

> Oh my dearest Lord, when the door to eternity is opened for me and I stand to be judged, I beg of you to judge me with love and not justice. For I could never stand in your justice and have my soul receive such a judgment. I would be quickly cast aside for I carry into eternity all my faults and weaknesses and the remains of a lifetime of sins and failures.

Such faults and weaknesses are ever present to the person; however, the person is not discouraged by them, nor do these weaknesses cause the person the anxiety they caused during the lower stages of union with God.

Many people in the lower stages of union with God become devastated when confronted with the results of their own human weaknesses. The main reason for that is that they have not as yet reached the level of the prayer life wherein they see themselves as being capable of having faults and weaknesses. To admit that to oneself takes a tremendous amount of grace and humility. Human nature, filled with self-love and pride, far too often looks outward trying to find someone else or some circumstance to blame when one falls into a sin or fault. That is clearly shown when, for example, an employer tells an employee that he has made a mistake. The first human reaction is to say: "Not me! Someone else made the mistake." Then comes the struggle to attempt to "prove" to others and to oneself that "someone else" did indeed make the mistake.

On the other hand many people are so discouraged by their own faults and weaknesses, that they tend to dislike themselves and feel that God could never love a person as "bad" as they imagine themselves to be.

Such problems never bother the person who has entered The Living Desert. Instead there is an amazing recovery from each fault or weakness. Why? Because by the time the person has entered The Desert, all mortal sins and numerous venial sins have been conquered. The faults and weaknesses which remain are used for the good of the soul and tend to make the person realize that she or he is still a human being, but a human being dearly loved by God in spite of faults and weaknesses.

In other words, the person has far more joy found in God's love than discouragement found in faults and weaknesses. The person's soul is surrounded by the eternal light and warmth of God's love; so much so, that the person could pen words like the following:

> Oh my dear Lord, if you look at me and judge me with pure love, then I can hide like a little child in your gaze and in your heart. Then I can speak to you of love and not about my many faults and failings.
>
> Please accept my love for you which I offer to you like a priceless jewel. For this love has the power to make sins, faults and weaknesses disappear within its glow.

Here you see how the person clearly views life as it is centered around Christ and His love. Yes, the faults and failings remain; however, the recovery from a little fall is so quick that these faults and failings cannot disturb the inner, wondrous peace and joy of a soul which has been allowed to taste the sweetness of being called into The Living Desert.

The person merely continues the day-by-day living knowing full well that his or her faults and weaknesses will surface now and then, but they quickly disappear in the fire of love: God's love for the person and the person's love for God.

Chapter 15

DEALING WITH REMAINING FAULTS AND WEAKNESSES

As I said in the last chapter, even in The Living Desert the person may still have human faults and weaknesses; however, the effects of these do not touch the inner depths of the soul. But even if the effects are not felt, how can the person deal with the knowledge that these faults remain?

The first way is to fully realize that these faults and weaknesses are a marvelous way to polish the precious virtue of humility. Nothing humbles a person more than to see themselves fall beneath the weight of a sin or fault which he or she believed had long ago vanished from the spiritual life. Some people are thrown into a state of turmoil when this happens but not a person who has entered The Living Desert. That is one sign that the person is in The Desert.

The person clearly sees his or her last remaining faults and weaknesses and admits that he or she is quite capable of having such faults and weaknesses. But now the person sees these faults and weaknesses in a different way than before. The person wishes to get rid of these, but in a different way than what was done in the lower states of the prayer life.

Now, whenever there is a slight fall into a fault or weakness, the person does not panic, nor are there spiritual battles to fight. The person instantly sees the mistake and goes about attempting to correct it in a state of pure peace and calmness. The person is actually amazed at how quickly the peace and calmness come but there is no mystery about that. The peace and calmness come because the effect of the faults and weaknesses cannot penetrate the chamber of peace and calmness the soul has entered. So there is no inner struggle or spiritual battle to fight.

At this point or stage of the spiritual development, the person does not have to "search" to find faults, nor struggle to overcome them. The fault is shown to the person and she or he knows what has to be done and does it quickly with no effort. There are no lingering doubts or fears or other spiritual turmoil. The person does not have "a million" conversations in order to try to convince herself or himself that she or he really didn't do anything wrong because. . .someone else can be blamed or some circumstances, etc., etc. In other words, the person no longer tries to justify her words or actions.

The person discovers that she or he has acquired a skill to quickly acknowledge a fault and, just as quickly, to learn the lesson Christ is attempting to teach her. Because, now, there is perfect cooperation between Christ and the person and the person allows Christ to guide her or him in all such matters. The person wants for its soul only what Christ wants. The two wills are bound together in a most remarkable way.

Also, the person does not want to waste any time or effort with such things as long, useless conversations with oneself because the person is so anxious to get her thoughts back to the Christ who dwells within The Desert in his or her soul.

The gifts of the Holy Spirit of wisdom, and knowledge, which include self-knowledge, are so highly polished that they act instantly to bring the soul up from the fall without the soul leaving the areas of spiritual peace and calmness.

Also, the person has absolutely no fears or worries about such falls or about the possibility of such falls. Although the person is fully aware that he or she is not perfect, the person knows that the One taking full command of the soul is. The person has so completely given her whole being to Christ that the person knows, without any doubts, that little falls would never harm the wondrous unity which the person now has with Christ.

The person, also, has a very precious way of dealing with such faults and weaknesses. It is called penance.

Penance becomes one of the greatest treasures given to the person, and he or she finds this treasure and knows how to use it.

While most people frown when penance is mentioned, the one who has reached The Living Desert prayer state cherishes each opportunity which presents itself so that a penance can be done. Such a penance does not have to be extraordinary or even painful. It can be as simple as picking up a piece of paper from the floor one does not have to do this. Sometimes just getting out of bed in the morning can become a penance.

But each and every act of penance can be done to wipe away the tarnish from a spiritual life caused by faults and weaknesses; if such is done with love.

The person who has entered The Living Desert, knows that if a fault is committed, a penance lovingly done is all that is necessary.

No matter how slight the fault, the person can instantly look for some act of penance to do so that the love-for-love relationship with Christ cannot suffer any damage in any way. That is why the person so loves and looks for each opportunity to do an act of penance; especially if a fault has been committed.

Chapter 16

THE LIVING DESERT AND CROSSES

Because I have described The Living Desert as bringing such peace and joy to the inner being of a person, it would seem to some that along with The Desert's joys there is an absence of troubles, problems, sufferings and crosses in daily life.

That conception would be a gross misunderstanding. What I said about The Living Desert state or stage of prayer is that inner, spiritual battles, sufferings, conflicts, darkness of soul, etc. vanish. There are no more struggles to pray, no more barriers separating the soul from Christ, no more doubts, worries or fears wondering if God really hears you when you pray, etc. There is only a tranquil, calm relationship with God as Christ is ever present, ever there, ever near and as the soul lives in the pure sunshine of His love and presence.

I did not say that material crosses, sufferings and problems disappear. But, someone may ask, how can a person be beset with material problems, sufferings and still have inner peace, joy and happiness? If someone has to ask that question then he or she has never experienced The Desert stage of the prayer life.

The answer to that question is simple, yet complex to anyone who has never experienced The Living Desert. The answer is to be found in the fact that The Desert exists within the inner core of the person's Christ-centered life. And when the person lives such a Christ-centered life, the cross stands there alongside of the heart.

By the time the person is called into The Desert, the person must of necessity have a very deep love for the crucified Christ and His cross. One cannot separate the cross from Christ for the cross became not only the way and means to our salvation, but the way and means to the very Heart of Christ. And if a person truly wants to follow Christ, he must do as Christ told us: "If anyone wishes to come after me, let him deny himself, take up his cross and follow me" (*Matthew* 16:24). Then, as the person advances spiritually and painfully climbs up each rung of THE LADDER OF PERFECTION, there comes that moment when the person fully understands and believes what Christ said about crosses: "Come to me, all you who labor and are burdened, and I will give you rest. Take my yoke upon you and learn from me for I am meek and humble of heart, and you will find rest for your souls. For my yoke is easy and my burden light" (*Matthew* 11:28-30). "Take my yoke upon you" for "my yoke is easy and my burden light." Think about those words. Millions of people have read them, even memorized them, but how many of these millions of people actually believed them? Did they really believe that the very cross of Christ, which He carried so faithfully, was a yoke and a burden light and easy to carry? And would all these millions, perhaps billions of people, accept Christ's own yoke and burden?

When the mother of John and James asked that her two sons sit next to Christ in His Kingdom, Christ asked: ". . .Can you drink of the cup of which I am about to drink?" (*Matthew* 20:20-22). They said to Him: "We can." But when Christ took these same two sons of Zebedee to the Garden of Gethsemani and said: "Sit down here, while I go over yonder and pray" (*Matthew* 26:36), these brave men who said they could drink the same cup Christ was about to drink, fell asleep: "Could you not then watch one hour with me?" (*Matthew* 26:39-40).

Carrying the same yoke Christ carried and drinking from the same cup of pain and agony which He drink from is a suffering beyond describing. Yet, Christ said His yoke would be "easy" to carry and His burden "light." Who could actually believe those words? But Christ said them. Not only did He expect us to believe them, but He told us to follow His bloody footsteps to the hill where upon there stood our own cross.

How can such a yoke and the burden of the cross be light and easy to carry? Christ gave us the answer: love.

By the time a person has entered The Living Desert, the person knows how to love Christ and to love the cross. Gone forever are the human reactions to crosses and sufferings. The ones which cause a person to hate sufferings, to ask: "Why did God do *this to me?*" or "What did I ever do to deserve this," etc.

In place of such natural complaints, there is a wondrous union of the soul with the crucified Christ and His cross. The person who has entered The Desert understands the cross and finds therein hidden treasures for the soul which will last forever. The person welcomes the opportunities of suffering for they unite the soul more closely to the crucified Savior. The person has the wisdom to be able to read the gold-edged book called the cross and find therein untold joys and sweetness because the person never removes the eyes of the soul from Christ.

When a person has entered The Desert, the person truly lives a Christ-centered life always seeing Christ, always loving Christ, always following Christ. The person never lowers his or her eyes, never allows Christ to fade from sight.

In *Matthew* 14:22-31, there is the story of Christ walking on the water. When Peter saw this miracle, he said to Christ: "Lord, if it is you, bid me come to you over the water." And Christ said: "Come." Then Peter got out of the boat and walked on the water to go to Jesus. But seeing that the wind was strong, he was afraid; and as he began to sink, he cried out saying, "Lord, save me!"

Peter was able to walk on the water as long as he looked at Christ. When he removed his glance from Christ and saw the situation he was in, he sank into the dark water.

When a person has entered The Living Desert, the person does not sink into the dark, muddy waters of despair and fear caused by sufferings because the person never removes the eyes of the soul from Christ. The person does not look away to see only the situation which exists. The person sees Christ and His cross *before* he sees his or her own and knows very well that no matter how heavy the burden is, love for Christ and His cross, makes the "yoke light" and "easy to carry." The person believes what Christ said.

When one has entered The Desert, the person never expects

crosses and sufferings to disappear. The person knows there will still be tears, heartache, even physical pain. But the person also knows something else which separates him or her from human complaints and rejection of crosses. The person knows there will be tears, yes, but not sadness. There will be heartache but not despair. There will be pain but not depression. Why? Because the light of love will always be shining.

It is love which is the secret of creating this spiritual "Garden of Eden" even if the person's material life is not such a garden.

Among all the trials and sufferings of life and living, the person, who has entered The Desert, can close his or her eyes and instantly the sweet, gentle, desert breeze of love refreshes the soul and brings an inner peace and joy which no cross or suffering can destroy.

Chapter 17

THE NEVER-ENDING DELIGHTS OF THE LIVING DESERT

Even though the person has entered The Living Desert state of union with God, the person has not reached the end or top of all spiritual goals. The final end is entrance into Heaven. However, as long as the person lives, there are more spiritual insights to gain and The Desert is alive with new and greater spiritual delights to experience.

The fact is, the person who has entered The Desert finds a most intense desire to allow Christ to continue to shape and mold his or her soul as He so desires. The soul is so alive with light and joy that it would be impossible to stop spiritual activity and prayer even if the person wanted to. Also, the person constantly searches for ways to express a deeper love for God through prayer, charity or carrying out daily duties and obligations.

Do not forget that Christ, who remains always in sight, has an infinite number of graces and spiritual treasures to bestow upon the soul. There is no end to the blessings and graces He can use to adorn the soul. He delights in the freedom given to Him by the person to continue to lavish His spiritual riches upon the soul He so dearly loves: and the soul waits anxiously for these gifts. The person has learned that by allowing Christ such freedom, he or she can receive added wondrous spiritual treasures which will last for all eternity.

The greatest of all these treasures is the increase of sanctifying grace. This grace is constantly being increased by prayer, the sacraments and living an active spiritual life. However, when the person enters The Desert, the increase of sanctifying grace goes far beyond what can be obtained in the lower or lesser stages of union with God. That is because the person's union with Christ is so free of all self-love and other barriers that nothing prevents the constant never-ending increase.

Often, spiritual barriers prevent a person from increasing sanctifying grace within his or her soul. If the person commits a mortal sin, such an increase can be delayed because now there is no longer any sanctifying grace to add to. If the person does not return to confession for years, then there can be no increase, no matter how many good deeds the person does or how faithfully he or she carries out daily duties and obligations.

Such spiritual problems do not exist when a person has entered The Living Desert. The reason being that the person's soul is always ready to have its sanctifying grace increased. The least glance towards Christ increases this grace as well as performing many acts of charity, praying long hours, receiving the sacraments faithfully and doing all sorts of penances.

As this grace increases, the union between Christ and the soul expands and intensifies. Such grace is needed in order to understand Christ better. The person's knowledge of Christ becomes greater and greater as He slowly reveals Himself, His ways, and His love to the soul now prepared to understand what the soul could not understand before.

As this grace increases, the person can begin to understand the way God acts, the way His love and mercy can be seen even when events seem so terrible, the way His justice is applied; all of which was so difficult to understand before.

The veils which prevented such understanding and which prompted remarks as: "Why did this happen to me?" or "What did I ever do to deserve this?" are removed. No longer does the person question or wonder about or try to find human answers for divine acts.

As can be well-imagined, the person, in such a spiritual situation, has a great deal of freedom from many normal, natural worries, fears, and anxieties. The person feels so secure within the blazing glow of the fire of love from the Sacred Heart of Christ that he or she puts into daily practice the prayer of holy abandonment to God's holy will.

And, still, with all these wondrous divine gifts which are given to the soul, there are yet more to be received by the soul which has the joys of being called into The Desert.

Chapter 18

THE FINAL STAGE OF THE LIVING DESERT: A LIVING PRAYER

After a person has lived The Living Desert state of union with God, there remains one final stage or state to enter into.

Although this final stage is part of The Desert, it is a totally new experience for the soul, one which the person never had before. It is also by far the sweetest, most beautiful stage of union with God. It is the crowning glory of the prayer life. I call it: A Living Prayer.

This state is so profound that only a very special grace from God allows the person to experience it and still live. It touches the very depths of the heart and soul. It is a complete, perfect fusion of the soul with God: one that will never break. No storms, sufferings or crosses of life could ever make this union disappear or cease to exist. No material distraction could distract the soul from the God who dwells within.

It is very difficult to explain this stage, but I will try to do it.

It is a spiritual state filled with immense, brilliant light which is so overpowering that the person often is able to see this light shine from within his or her being and spread outward.

Not only does this inner light radiate outward from the depths of the soul, but this light becomes a shield or screen which protects the soul in a most miraculous way from any and all outside influences which could break the soul's union with God. The person actually feels this shield of protection and his or her whole being is filled with tremendous joy. At any given moment, among all sorts of material situations (working, carrying crosses, etc.)

the person has only to close his or her eyes, enter The Living Desert, and see the brilliant light flowing outward, in a never-ending stream, from the depths of the soul.

No matter what the person does, as he or she faithfully carries out the duties and obligations of daily life, the person knows, without any doubts, that this light of grace shines forth, always bright, always warm, always filled with indescribable sweetness. And that makes the person A Living Prayer.

One day Our Lord appeared to a friend of St. Gertrude the Great and He said: "I so love Gertrude because as she goes about her daily duties, she never takes her eyes off of me." That is what I mean by being A Living Prayer. The eyes of the soul never look away from Christ. He is always in clear focus. There is nothing between the person and the object of his or her affection: no distractions, no desires, no spiritual barriers. And that look of love becomes a constant, never-ending prayer.

The person never wanders away from God nor the light of His grace. This spiritual state is far greater than merely doing God's holy will. For one can do God's holy will and at the same time, have her soul beset with all sorts of troubles and spiritual problems. Being A Living Prayer means to exist in total inner solitude where nothing disturbs nor distracts the soul. It is a wondrous feeling not only of being aware that the person is never out of the sight of God but God is never out of the sight of the person.

The person feels that he or she has been put into a container of God's pure love and that all earthly, material distractions have disappeared. However, at the same time, life goes on as usual, daily work is done, crosses come and go, etc. But among all the ways of living a human life, the soul constantly sings a sweet love song to God and hears His sweet love song in perfect tune with the soul's. That is being A Living Prayer.

Then, when the person retires to a place of solitude for prayer, the rapture of the soul's union with God makes prayer so easy, so filled with joy, so overwhelming that often words are not necessary. All forms of prayer can enter into the prayer time, vocal, mental, and contemplation. However, the person feels that all words are incased in the glowing brilliance of the light of grace which flows constantly from the hidden depths of the soul's union with God and the person drifts "in and out" of the silent rapture of light and pure, holy love while praying. When words are not said, the light of love becomes so spiritually illuminating that such a love says everything. The person has to only love and God does the rest. He hears all, He knows all, and He only looks for the opportunities, given to Him by the person, to lavish upon the soul the finest and greatest spiritual treasures.

After this final stage of The Living Desert has been entered into, there remains only one more stage: Heaven. Then the soul becomes A Living Prayer for all eternity. A person who has reached this final stage of The Desert can lovingly cry out to God:

> Oh, my dearest Lord, I am wrapped completely in the glowing furnace of your love. I am taken out of my human senses into the areas of divine love and light. My whole being rises to embrace the light of your nearness and love.
>
> I am no longer a lonely pilgrim on earth, but a being made holy by your light and grace. My poor crust of a human cover for my soul is melting away from my soul for I seek treasures more precious than material well-being and comforts. I cannot rest until my soul, made restless by its quest for perfect union with you, has, at last, reached is goal: Heaven.

PART FOUR

HEAVEN, OUR GOAL

Chapter 1

HEAVEN, OUR GOAL

Any person who seeks to climb THE LADDER OF PERFEC-
TION has to know and believe that the top of THE LADDER reaches right into Heaven. Heaven then becomes the goal and also the
fulfillment of one's desires to reach a very close union with God.
If a person truly desires complete union with God, the perfection
of that union has to be Heaven where one actually sees the object
of his or her affection face-to-face. No longer will a person have
to think about being with God, the person will *be* with God, not
just for a day or a month or a year but for all eternity.

No longer will the person have to try and imagine what it
means to be caught up, forever, in the wonder of God's love, the
person will experience such. The veil of life will be drawn aside
and the person will see the wondrous beauties they could not
even imagine existed while on earth.

Heaven then becomes the goal to reach, our dream-come-true,
the grandest adventure of a created human's entire existence. Yet,
strange as it sounds, a vast number of people cannot accept the
idea that they were created to know God, to love God and to be
happy with Him forever in His eternal Heaven of love, peace, joy
and happiness. These people say they believe that a Heaven
exists, however, they have a very difficult time accepting the
notion that they will one day go there.

I am not talking about great sinners who do nothing for God or
for their own souls. I am talking about people who believe in
God, love Him, pray to Him, go to Church, receive the sacraments and love the Holy Mother of God.

Often such people will make remarks such as: "I want to go to

Heaven, but I am not sure I will make it." Or: "I am trying to go to Heaven but really I don't know if I am doing what I should be doing to get there." Or: "I know my mother is in Heaven, but I am not sure that some day I will be there myself."

In and by such remarks, there can clearly be seen a sign of their lack of religious knowledge. If they really understood their Catholic faith and God, they would know that the sanctifying grace given to their souls by Holy Mother Church through the sacraments makes it possible for them to reach Heaven and that God, Himself, desires ardently that they use such grace and faith from their redemption to save their souls. Christ gave His life so that they can one day be happy with Him in Heaven for all eternity. This death opened the gates of Heaven.

A Catholic should at all times know that his or her soul is in the state of grace. There should be no guesswork about such an important fact. One's soul is in the state of grace when mortal sin is not present. If a person commits a mortal sin, he or she should immediately go to confession. When the soul receives sanctifying grace, then the soul can one day enter Heaven. A soul in the state of grace is a soul saved. A person does not have to wonder if he will or will not enter Heaven. If the soul is in the state of grace, the person *can know* that one day Heaven's joys will be his. The idea is not to keep wondering if Heaven will be reached, but to make sure that one's soul is at all times in the state of grace.

It is not pride to stand firm in the grace of God and to say: "As long as God's grace fills my soul with His presence and light I know I will be saved."

That is the secret of knowing if you will or will not go to Heaven. You must understand grace and what grace does for your soul.

A newly baptized person, infant or adult, would go immediately to Heaven if death follows. How can we be sure? Because grace, sanctifying grace, is what is needed in order to enter the kingdom of Heaven and a baptized person has this grace. In exactly the same way, any person whose soul has sanctifying grace, has a soul that will be saved. If a person pays attention to the grace within his or her own soul, that person can be sure of going to Heaven as long as sanctifying grace floods the soul with God's light and grace; even if some time is to be spent in Purgatory.

Going to Heaven is not just something which comes from without as some sort of a reward for a good deed. It is not something which we have no control over, like getting a prize for the best painting or having your lucky number pulled out of a hat. We do have control over our own personal salvation (or going to Heaven). Within our own free will lies the key to our salvation. With this key, we open the gates of Heaven and walk in. If we truly want to go to Heaven, if we protect God's grace within our souls by not committing mortal sins (or by going to Confession to restore grace after a mortal sin has been committed), if we follow the teachings of Christ and of the Church, if we have faith and trust in God, we will save our souls. There will be no doubts; we will go to Heaven. If we do not "make it," if we throw away the grace necessary for salvation, the fault will be entirely ours, not God's or someone else's. We are the only ones who can take the detour away from God's grace and Heaven. No one can take Heaven away from us as long as our souls are in the state of grace, and we do God's holy will: prayer, the sacraments, etc.

When someone says that he or she is "not sure" of going to Heaven, the person usually means that he or she does not understand the grace of God within his or her own soul. Anyone who understands the purpose of sanctifying grace, knows also that if death strikes, he will be saved and he will go to Heaven. Having such confidence in the power of God's grace is by no means being proud. It is the kind of faith and trust which God requires of us.

All the doubts and fears concerning personal salvation (and sometimes these doubts can become a true torture) will disappear once the person has a clear understanding of sanctifying grace. Many people do not have such an understanding. I know many people who live a good Catholic life, who go to Mass and the sacraments; but who still say: "I hope that some day I will be saved."

It must be remembered that salvation is not a "hit or miss" type of a situation. In other words, people do not stand in a long line waiting for someone to choose who will or will not enter the "pearly gates." The person, himself, accepts or rejects Heaven by and through an acceptance or rejection of sanctifying grace. If this grace is wanted and used and kept alive in a soul, the person will be saved.

It is also interesting, as well as enlightening, to know that many people think that God does not want them in Heaven. This is false humility at its height. Many people have said to me: "How could I be saved; I am such a sinner. God doesn't want me!"

I answer by explaining that the whole story of salvation history (the reason for the Redemption) was because God so loved and wanted sinners. Some of the first words which Christ spoke were: "It is not the healthy who need a physician but they who are sick. For I have not come to call the just, but sinners" (*Mark* 2:17).

If a person feels that he or she is such a "sinner" that salvation is impossible, the fault lies within the person's own free will. Sinners we all are; however, sanctifying grace is available to all sinners. A sincere, valid confession restores this grace to a soul if mortal sin destroyed such grace. Once the soul is in the state of grace, Heaven awaits the person if death strikes.

God so loved sinners that He not only sent His beloved Son to die upon the cross for sinners; but He left to us the Sacrament of Reconciliation (Confession). He wants us in Heaven with Him. We have only to make the effort to get there. If we fail, it will be our fault, not God's.

So Heaven is within the reach of all of us. We can be sure that we will "make it" if we work for our salvation every day. But please remember that being sure of going to Heaven, by keeping your soul in the state of grace, has nothing to do with the sin of presumption. Some people like to believe that they will go to Heaven "in the end," "God will forgive me, He understands," no matter what they do, no matter how many sins they commit. That, of course, is not true; and such presumption is a sin. Such people, who like to believe that they will be saved, no matter what they do, no matter what sins they commit, care nothing about grace nor the condition of their own souls. Such people will not repent nor give up sinful ways. That is not confidence in the power of grace, that is to boldly presume that one will be saved without a spiritual conversion.

The kind of confidence I am speaking about comes from

knowing and understanding the power of sanctifying grace; but more, using this grace so that you can be sure you will indeed go to Heaven.

The fact is, it is wise to keep Heaven as your highest goal in life. Each day a person should make a completely spiritual examination to make sure that his or her soul is in the state of grace. If a person is not sure, then a confessor can help with this problem. When a person has sanctifying grace, then he or she is in union with God, and this union with God will last forever in Heaven.

It is very important to remember that Heaven is gained by the person's cooperation with grace and through faith. That puts the person's salvation within his or her own abilities. In other words, man, himself, earns Heaven with his own free will by and through living an active spiritual life and accepting the truths (doctrines) of Christ. A person does not *just go* to Heaven, but attains this blessed state through holy acts of love for God, prayer, charity, faith, the sacraments, etc. Christ opened the way to salvation by His death upon the cross: however, man must cooperate with Christ's saving grace. Because of that fact, Heaven becomes a more blessed and glorious state simply because man obtained it with the freedom of his own will. Even a sinner who saves his or her soul upon a deathbed, earns Heaven through a humble, sincere act of the will.

Now, what will Heaven be like? First of all, what will we look like? One day a friend of mine began to ask his relatives and friends what they thought their own souls looked like. He received an amazing assortment of unexpected answers. Some said that the soul was merely a "puff of smoke." Others said that their souls were a "cloud" that had no form. Still others remarked that the soul was a "ghost." Each person was surprised when told that the soul was the person, with arms, legs, etc. He or she would reply: "I didn't know that!"

How do we learn that the soul of each person looks exactly like the person and is not just a "puff of smoke"? The best way to see this truth is to remember Christ's Ascension and Mary's Assumption. Christ and His holy mother both went to Heaven body and soul. Their glorified bodies are in Heaven. They look like they did while on earth. If the holy men and women and even angels did not look like humans with arms, legs, etc., then Christ and Mary would be totally out of place in Heaven with their bodies. Also, we are made into the image and likeness of God. We know what God looks like, as far as a body with arms and legs is concerned, because we know that Christ who was God had a human body. So, in Heaven we will look like a human person and be able to recognize our loved ones, our relatives and our friends who will look like they did while on earth, except they will be filled with the light and beauty of holy souls in Heaven.

Holy Scripture has many passages which tell us that we will not lose our human shape in Heaven. Christ said: "Let not your heart be troubled. You believe in God, believe also in me. In my Father's house there are many mansions. Were it not so, I should have told you because I go to prepare a place for you. And if I go and prepare a place for you, I am coming again and I will take you to myself; that where I am, there you also may be. . .if you had known me, you would also have known my Father; and henceforth, you do know Him and you have seen Him" (*John* 14:1-7). When Philip said to Him, "Lord, show us the Father," Jesus quickly replied: ". . .Philip, he who sees me sees also the Father. . ." (*John* 14:8-9).

What need would a human being have of a "mansion" in Heaven or a place prepared by Christ, if this human being turned into a "puff of smoke" in Heaven?

At the Last Supper, Christ said: ". . .but I say to you, I will not drink henceforth of this fruit of the vine, until that day when I shall drink it new with you in the kingdom of my Father" (*Matthew* 26:29).

When Adam and Eve saw and spoke to the Lord God in the Garden of Eden, God had a human shape (but He was not a human being), the "same image" which He created man to resemble: ". . .when they heard the sound of the Lord God walking in the garden. . .the man and his wife hid themselves. . .(and the man said) 'I heard you in the garden and I was afraid. . .'" (*Genesis* 3:8-10).

Now, what will Heaven be like, this wondrous goal we are all striving for?

Chapter 2

A CLOSER LOOK AT HEAVEN

In this chapter and the following one, I would like to open up Heaven so that we can take a closer look at it, and have a better understanding of what God's eternal home is like.

Although Saint Paul told us that: "Eye has not seen or ear heard, nor has it entered into the heart of man, what things God has prepared for those who love Him" (*1 Corinthians* 2:9), there is a great deal which we do know about Heaven. We obtain such information from Holy Scripture and from the teachings of our Church.

However, because of the nature of this book, I do not have to write a long chapter on Heaven to try and convince you that there is a Heaven. We know, when we are climbing THE LADDER OF PERFECTION, that the ladder reaches upward toward Heaven. Heaven, which is living with God in His home for all eternity, becomes our goal.

Heaven then becomes for the spiritual person, the fulfillment of desires which had been planted in him when he built his platform upon which THE LADDER OF PERFECTION rests.

A person can climb a mountain just "because it's there." When the top is reached, he can have the satisfaction of knowing he reached his goal. He can shout to the world: "I did it, I did it." However, he must then turn around to descend that same mountain. He cannot stay at the top because up there is a very big "nothing." It is empty space where he cannot find the necessities for human survival.

Not so, when one climbs THE LADDER OF PERFECTION. Once one has reached the top, he can stay there, he does not have to descend. Why? Because the top of the ladder is Heaven, the everlasting goal is reached. A new life of magnificent peace, joy and happiness has been gained and this life will last for all eternity.

The fact that the top of the ladder is Heaven becomes a truth filled with all the hope and encouragement one needs as he or she struggles to climb that ladder. If only a vast nothingness existed at the top of the ladder, no one would want to spend a lifetime struggling up the slippery rungs.

The very first efforts we make, when we start our climb tell us that we long for the fulfillment of our goal, which is to have a very close, precious union with God in His Heaven of love. That has to be our motive, that has to be the call of conversion heard deep within our souls. We have to, not only have faith in the existence of Heaven, we have to know that God made us for the sublime union with Him in His home; and the more we know and love Him on earth, the more we will know and love Him in Heaven. (That knowledge and love increase with an increase of sanctifying grace.)

While on earth, we can only catch a tiny glimpse of the realities of Heaven; however, that brief view obtained through grace and faith, is enough to have us realize that earth is merely a stopover place in our whole existence as a human being with a soul. So, the struggle up THE LADDER OF PERFECTION is not the beginning and the end of holiness but the way to a pure, holy love for God which we will express in Heaven for all eternity.

Yet, often the ones who sincerely want to go to Heaven do not understand very much about this eternal state of joy.

In one way, it is very foolish to spend a lifetime struggling against the world, the flesh and the devil so as to enter Christ's home; and at the same time, have no idea what Heaven is all about. Why? Because if one does not realize certain facts about Heaven, the person cannot create for himself the fullest of heavenly joys. So, I wish to explain what we can do now to enter into a more complete, perfect union with Christ in His Heaven of love with more joys and even more glory.

Most people have a preconceived notion about Heaven and

what happens there. This idea or knowledge is usually very limited and very narrow. Most people think of Heaven as being only one big place filled with eternal joy and happiness. Some people put limits upon Heaven by imagining that Heaven is doing things like singing songs or playing harps for all eternity.

Well, Heaven is a place of eternal joy and happiness and people there (or souls) do sing and perhaps angels do play harps, however, Heaven is far more than such limited ideas about it.

The main trouble or problem with people's ideas about Heaven is that they, more or less, think about it in a one-sentence type of description. In other words, they can describe Heaven with only a few words such as there exists Heaven, Hell and earth. Earth is here. Heaven is up there and Hell is down there. That is all, nothing more: "When I die, I want to go to Heaven. That is all I have to know about it."

As a result, because of such meager, poor knowledge about Heaven, many people do not have any desires to go there. So we hear such foolish remarks as: "Why bother to save your soul because Heaven will be nothing more than an eternity of dull, boring events." Or, "Who wants to play a harp for all eternity?" Some really foolish people make unfunny jokes about Heaven and say: "I would rather go to Hell where all my friends are!" (I am glad I am not one of the "friends.")

Other people want to believe that Heaven is merely a reward for belief in God or in Christ. Some false religions actually teach that as long as a person says "I believe in Christ" that is all that is needed for salvation. But that is not true. Faith in God is the beginning of salvation, but living a life filled with grace and virtue, doing what Christ tells us to do, accepting His holy will for us; all must become a vital part of saving our souls. Saint Paul tells us: "Life eternal, indeed, He will give to those who by patience in good works seek glory and honor and immortality" (*Romans* 2:7).

Heaven then becomes, not so much a reward for belief in Christ but the goal to reach or the success found after a long struggle up the mountain of perfection.

Many people, who have a very limited knowledge or a distorted idea about Heaven, fail to realize that they themselves are in control of situations which could lead them to the heights of that mountain. As I said, Heaven is the goal to reach, and the struggles begin while the person is still on earth. One does not reach Heaven merely by dying and going there. One must struggle to reach that lofty goal every moment of every day.

To say that the struggle is worth it, is to put it mildly. Just think about the way an athlete will struggle, train, endure all sorts of pains and sufferings and never give up even after many failures along the way, just for the honor and prestige of winning a gold medal at the Olympic Games. But all too soon the glory and honor fades as someone else takes his or her place as the "greatest in the world."

Then, what about the ones who suffered just as much, training for 10 or 12 years, for that one glorious moment of winning the gold medal but who fail? Someone else is just a little bit better or a second faster or a bit more precise. What a monumental disappointment! "The agony of defeat" are correct words to describe that feeling. All hopes are gone. There is no "second chance." All is wasted as something ends which had consumed the person day and night for years.

Whenever I see an athlete in training for the Olympic Games on a T.V. program, it never ceases to amaze me how much effort and time he or she spends ever seeking that illusive gold medal. I say to myself: "It would be wonderful if he spent as much time working for God and gaining merits for Heaven, what a glorious eternity he would have." Just like the person who climbed the mountain and then must turn around to descend, so will the person, who seeks the Olympic gold and fails, have to descend from the heights of his or her ambition into the valley of defeat.

Not so when one climbs THE LADDER OF PERFECTION to the glorious heights of Heaven. For this person there is no failure and always the gold medal of success awaits.

But what exactly is the success of actually reaching Heaven? Will it be just a place filled with angels playing harps or will it be the glories of a magnificent sunrise which will never fade and which one will never tire of watching?

First of all, Heaven will be for each soul there a very personal, private experience of untold joy and happiness. One will be totally and completely encased in the presence of God and His infinite love. Heaven will be the state of perfection, the final and complete steps taken up THE LADDER OF PERFECTION.

We will know ourselves perfectly and at the same time know the answers to all the mysteries of our life on earth which we could never completely understand. We will see and understand the way God blessed us, protected us, watched over us, gave to us the abilities we possessed, abilities of body, heart, soul, intellect, will and understanding.

We will find everything about the glories of Heaven ever new, ever thrilling, ever exciting.

Heaven is also a place of pure, holy, infinite love. Everyone will love us as God loves us and we, in turn, will love all who dwell in God's home with a love completely and perfectly free of any trace of self-love or self-seeking motives.

Imagine, if you can, being filled with so much love for billions of people that you will want to know each one personally and share their joys and happiness. Indeed, it would take all eternity to accomplish such, but you will have all eternity to seek out and learn about all who dwell with you in God's own kingdom.

Imagine, also if you can, the total perfection of many things you see on earth. Remember that earth is a reflection, often a distorted reflection, but nevertheless a reflection of Heaven. Imagine trees, grass and flowers which will never dry up and die, birds that will never stop singing, magnificent lakes or rivers. Try to think of the most perfect of such things and still you can only catch a tiny glimpse of the wondrous beauties of Heaven.

Imagine being surprised, not once or twice, but "a million times" with precious little gifts from those who dearly love you. Imagine sharing, with the ones you have known and loved on earth, all sorts of delightful, happy moments, like being together at a wedding feast which will never end.

Imagine being engaged in all sorts of holy, good, occupations or tasks which can give to you a perfect feeling of satisfaction as you ever delight in pleasing God, and His holy Mother Mary, as well as others whom you might serve for all eternity, such as a great saint. Imagine that you, yourself, could have surrounding you, faithful friends or loved ones whose greatest, eternal joy will be just to be near you and do things to please you or to serve you.

Imagine all the things I just mentioned and still you cannot fully imagine the wondrous joys and surprises which the good Lord plans to bestow upon you when you are home, at last, in the place where you can dwell for all eternity in perfect peace, joy and happiness with people you love and who will love you.

Heaven then is a state of eternal, pure, holy joy and bliss, a never-ending feast given for and by God's elect. Needless to say, in this eternal state of pure joy and bliss, there will be no sorrow, no death, no suffering, no arguments, no sins such as jealousy, pride, lust and so forth. Never again can a person fall to human weaknesses and faults. Human nature will be perfected so that all in Heaven will possess holy virtues and grace.

As wondrous as will be all I have described about Heaven, the most marvelous gift found in Heaven will be the ability to see God face-to-face, to see His splendor and glory. It will be like looking at the most beautiful picture one could ever imagine and never tiring of gazing upon the supreme beauty and exquisite loveliness of what the eye, heart and mind behold.

Not only will the eye, mind and heart see the beauty and splendor of God, but the person will come to know God, His ways, His love, mercy and justice as could never be known and understood on earth. Then there will come the awe-struck realization of knowing that for all eternity never will one lose sight of God, never will He be gone, never will He cease to love and be loved.

We will find ourselves, in Heaven, in a land of perfect beauty, joy and love where we can live for all eternity. We will no longer need faith to tell us that such a home exists, we will be there and we will stay there forever, always experiencing the wonders and joys of God's love for us and our love for Him.

Chapter 3

THE DIFFERENT DEGREES OF GLORY
IN HEAVEN

As I said in the last chapter, the goal or fulfillment of one's climb up THE LADDER OF PERFECTION is Heaven. That goal should always be kept in mind, especially during the many days of discouragement which do occur as one struggles up that ladder.

However, as important as it is to keep the goal of Heaven always in mind, there is something else which is just as important to keep in mind. That "something" concerns the different degrees of glory found in Heaven.

Not only is the final act of perfection, which is one's total, perfect union with Christ in Heaven, always our aim, but we must remember that we also must strive for a deeper love and understanding of Christ who will greet us when we reach our home with Him. This deeper love and understanding means a greater degree of glory for ourself.

Very, very few people realize that in Heaven there are numerous degrees or stages of glory. Yet, to have different degrees of glory is only plain common sense. Surely a great sinner, who was converted and who saved his or her soul upon the deathbed, could never enjoy the same amount of glory or happiness or love nor could the person understand God as does a great saint or the holy Mother of God. They could not all exist for all eternity on the same level of union with God. Why? Because not only do people earn Heaven by living a life of grace, they also earn their own level of eternal union with God. In other words, everyone has within his own power the ability to rise to what I call a "higher" Heaven or to remain upon a lower level of Heaven, or the lowest which I call the "Heaven of no Merit."

Holy Mother Church is very positive in her teaching that there are different degrees of love and happiness in Heaven. Christ told us that fact. In *Matthew* 5:17-19, Christ said: ". . .insignificant of these commands and teaches others to do so, shall be called the least in the kingdom of God. Whoever fulfills and teaches these commands shall be great in the kingdom of God."

He also refers to such degrees of glory when He told the parable of the wedding feast. He explained the fact that if a person goes to the head of the table, when not asked, he will be put into the lowest place (*Luke* 14:8-11).

It is very logical and reasonable to believe that the more the soul is purified on earth, the more that sanctifying grace is increased within the soul, the higher degree of holiness a person reaches, the higher degree of happiness and love will be his or hers for all eternity.

The degree of happiness or glory which a person attains in Heaven depends a great deal upon the amount of sanctifying grace within the soul when the person dies. It is grace which brings to us the ability to know, love and understand God. That is why a person who dies in a state of mortal sin cannot enter Heaven, and even if he could, he would be totally incapable of understanding God or His love. That being the case, it can be clearly seen that the more we increase sanctifying grace, the greater will be our understanding of God and His love. This greater understanding will increase our happiness and glory when we enter God's home.

Saint Teresa of Avila said that she would not mind staying on earth, suffering greatly, until the end of time if by that means she could increase her love for God just a tiny bit more.

Now to understand this teaching more fully, first of all, realize that just because one person in Heaven may have far more glory and happiness than someone else that does not mean that the person with a lesser degree of happiness will be deliberately denied the greater degree. It does not mean that God is more generous to a favorite son or daughter with His heavenly treasures and with-holds these same treasures from others. If that were the case, then it would mean that God would, in a sense, punish a person who did not show Him enough love on earth.

No matter what level of glory or happiness a person will be upon in Heaven, within that level will be all that the person could ever desire for all eternity. In other words, everyone in Heaven, no matter upon which level the person will find his or her eterni-ty, will exist in a state of total, complete joy and happiness and will receive all the eternal treasures which were earned and per-haps a few more from the infinite generosity of a loving Father.

In other words, a person not only creates for himself his eter-nal destiny, which may be Heaven, Hell or Purgatory, but a per-son also creates for himself the degree of happiness or glory in Heaven. God does not withhold treasures from certain people in Heaven, God merely gives to a person all which the person had created for himself. If this "all" is a lot less than say the treasures given to a great saint, it is the person who is at fault and not God. That is why it is so important to constantly increase one's sancti-fying grace, which in turn will increase one's love for and under-standing of God, which in turn will increase one's union with God, which in turn will increase one's eternal glory.

Heaven is indeed eternal happiness for all who will live there, but not all eternal happiness is the same. Heaven is eternal union with God, to see Him face-to-face, but not all in Heaven will see God in the same way. Heaven is to know and understand God, however, not everyone in Heaven will know and understand Him in the same way. Heaven is to love God, but not everyone in Heaven will love Him in the highest degree of love. Heaven is filled with eternal delights and treasures, but not all in Heaven share the same delights and treasures.

Why? Because not everyone who saves his or her soul reaches the same levels or heights of love for God and perfection while on earth. Not everyone who enters the celestial portals walked there-in with the same amount of sanctifying grace. Not everyone, while on earth, created for himself the same eternal degree of happiness or glory. It is what you do now, while alive, that will bring to you a greater or a lesser degree of eternal happiness and glory.

Let me explain this another way.

In all walks of life and in all types of living, there are many different degrees of education, abilities, intellects, etc. Many people possess talents which others do not. There are even different classes of people: the poor, the middle-income, the wealthy, etc. Billions of people live on earth, but not all live in the same way; so why should one imagine that in Heaven, billions of people will be in exactly the same eternal state or degree of happiness and love for God?

Now, when a person fully realizes the fact that there are indeed different degrees or levels of happiness and glory in Heaven, it makes good sense for the person to have as his or her goal a "higher" Heaven instead of "merely saving one's soul" and entering into a "lesser" or lower level of Heaven. As someone once said to me: "Why settle for the least amount of glory and happiness when one can reach a higher Heaven?"

Now, there are two questions which could be asked once a person understands that not all souls in Heaven exist on the same levels of glory and happiness. The first question is: "Why would anyone want a level higher than the lowest? Is it not more important to just get to Heaven than to worry about what level one will reach in Heaven?" The second question is: "If I do try to reach a higher level would not that be very vain and presumptuous on my part?"

I will answer the first question by saying that the most important task of all is indeed to save one's soul and to be assured of an eternity of joy and happiness in God's home. That is why the Church teaches that it is possible for the greatest of sinners to save his soul on his deathbed at the last moment of life. And we can believe that a vast majority of sinners do indeed save their souls at the last moment. We can also believe that such souls, when they finally reach Heaven, will be completely satisfied for all eternity with the least amount of glory and bliss. One of their greatest joys will be found in knowing they are a saved soul.

But, let me now talk about a person who earned a higher degree of glory. The person was faithful to God most if not all of his or her life. Prayers were said and much love was given to God by this person. What is the difference between the glory of such a soul compared to a person who committed dreadful sins, gained no merits or spiritual treasures and just barely managed to save his soul on his deathbed? The best way to show this difference is to tell the following little story.

A child, aged about 6 or 7 years is taken to see an art exhibit by his mother, who is accompanied by an expert art critic. Here we have three different people on three different levels of intellect, knowledge and understanding. I will add that the three are also examples of a very wide gap concerning love for art. Surely the child and the mother could never love exquisite paintings to the same degree of intensity as does the critic whose whole life is centered around art.

The three stand in front of one of the world's greatest paintings. What is each one's reaction?

The little child will look and not really see or understand what is before his eyes. Then he will suddenly notice a dog next to the feet of a king. The child will be thrilled and become very excited. He will find his complete enjoyment of the painting merely by seeing the dog and understanding what a dog is.

The mother will find her complete enjoyment of the painting by noticing the beautiful clothes worn by the figures in the painting or the room which is richly decorated.

However, the art critic will notice and enjoy much more. He will admire the skill of the painter. He will notice the play of brilliant colors, shadows, lines and composition of the painting. He will marvel at the intricate details of the figures in the painting, the flow of garments, the expressions on the faces, the position of the hands, the details of designs in the garments, the painting of the hair. He will know that the artist painted a table, a flower and even the dog with just as much care as he did his main subjects in the painting.

The critic's understanding and knowledge, as well as his love for art, will give him a far greater degree of enjoyment when viewing the painting than could ever be received by the child or the child's mother.

Now transfer that example to the different degrees of love for, union with, and understanding of God in Heaven.

An adult who never increased sanctifying grace in his or her soul, or an adult who saved his soul only upon his deathbed, has to be compared to possessing an intellect, knowledge and understanding of a small child when that person views God in Heaven and will, in a sense, have a child's level of eternal happiness.

On the other hand, a person, a great saint, acquired so much grace while on earth that this person will be able to understand and love God in a far superior way and thus enjoy a far greater degree of eternal glory.

So, as my friend said: Why settle for only a child's level of eternal joy and happiness? Why love and understand God only with the love and understanding of a child, when a person has within his or her power the ability to love and understand God for all eternity as a great saint will? Why settle for a low level or degree of eternal glory when a person can rise to a higher level?

That brings up the second question I asked. Will it be or is it selfish or vain to desire a greater degree of eternal happiness and glory? The answer is, no! Why? Because it is God's will that we accept all the spiritual treasures and glory which He desires to give to us. He has an infinite amount of spiritual treasures which He not only has, but which He wants us to possess. He wants to see us dressed in the finest eternal garments, and be in the highest levels of eternal glory. When we do reach such heights, then we will have the ability to give greater glory and love to God. In other words, the greater our glory is in Heaven, the more glory and pleasure we give to God.

For example: Imagine if you can, a loving father who loves to have deep, intellectual, meaningful talks with an older, adult child who will completely understand all He tells the child rather than with a small youngster who does not have the capability to understand what he is talking about. Surely the father would receive far more pleasure telling all his thoughts and secrets to the child who will be able to understand these thoughts and secrets. While the little one can also give the father pleasure and joy, the father is in need of the happiness given to him by his talks with a child who understands all his ways.

In like manner, a person whose soul has, through living a very holy life a tremendous amount of grace can bring far more glory and pleasure to the heavenly Father than someone who entered Heaven with no merits and only the grace necessary for eternal salvation.

No, it is not vain or selfish to desire and strive for a greater glory in Heaven. It is God's will that you do so; because He has the desires to bestow upon His beloved children numerous spiritual treasures. It is the gathering of these treasures which determines the amount of glory one will have for all eternity.

Chapter 4

GRACE AND ETERNAL HAPPINESS

As I said in the last chapter, your personal Heaven and the degree of happiness and union with God which shall be given to you will be determined by the amount of grace and perfection your soul gained on its journey toward eternity. In other words, your eternal level or degree of joy and happiness lies within your own power to create while you are still on earth. God, of course, will have the right to increase what you have obtained; however, basically what you do now as you strive for perfection will place you upon the level of eternal joy which you built for yourself.

One time a soul from Purgatory appeared to a saintly nun. The nun asked the soul if families will be together and know each other in Heaven. The holy soul explained that in Heaven members of the same family are not always together because people do not merit the same rewards. In other words, each person receives as an eternal reward, the joy and happiness which he or she merits or gains while on earth.

Eternal happiness in itself, even the least or lesser type, far exceeds the most wondrous happiness and joy on earth. Words cannot really describe the type of joy which flows constantly over each soul in Heaven, even the souls in the "Heaven of no Merit." Within this lowest level, souls experience waves of bliss and happiness which cover them with an eternal peace and contentment. If a soul were to stay in the lowest, smallest corner of Heaven for all eternity, that soul would find enough joy to be completely satisfied for all eternity and would never desire a greater joy. Their one most glorious feeling is to know that they were not lost and they can see God face-to-face for all eternity. Just being able to see God face-to-face for all eternity and to exist in His infinite love is reward enough for anyone.

Yet, God has an infinite assortment of heavenly treasures to add to that gift of His presence and love which He is ready to give to souls who have acquired greater merit while on earth. And He desires souls to take unto themselves these treasures.

As I said, it is not selfish to work to gain a share of these treasures. God's desire to give us treasures can be compared to a wealthy man who desires to give only the best of gifts to his beloved children. If one of his children refuses the gifts, that makes him sad because his greatest joy is to see his children dressed in the finest garments, living in the best surroundings. Such children bring him immense pleasure and are a testimony of his care and love for them. But if one of his children rejects his gifts and wants to live in a rebellious, slanderous way, that child gives him no joy, pleasure or glory. That child becomes a cross.

In like manner, the more we allow God to dress us in the finest spiritual garments of grace and heavenly treasures, the more joy and glory we give to Him, the more He is pleased with us, and the closer will be our union with Him in Heaven.

The secret of receiving from God more and greater eternal treasures is increasing sanctifying grace which is needed to climb higher up THE LADDER OF PERFECTION. Christ not only gave us saving grace (sanctifying grace) by and through His redemptive act, He also makes available to us a vast, never-ending amount of eternal treasures which we can find in and through the increase of this saving grace.

God did not create His children only for the purpose of bestowing upon them the eternal joys and happiness of Heaven. God made them so that they can not only reach Heaven, but go there, through good and pious acts of prayer and charity, filled with numerous eternal treasures which will add to eternal happiness and glory.

What loving father would not want to have all his children share his most precious treasures? God, being not only our

Father but the infinite Father, desires us to share His most precious treasures for all eternity. However, He cannot bestow upon anyone treasures which they do not want or which they reject. That would be like a father on earth trying to force his treasures upon the rebellious son who does not want anything to do with his father or his wealth. Man still has a free will which God will not interfere with.

Heaven then can become more blessed, more filled with happiness, joy and love because man can earn such an increase in happiness, joy and love with his own free will through meritorious acts. Such acts are prayer, receiving the sacraments, charity, penance, obedience to the teachings of Christ and the Church, etc. All gain eternal merits. As great as the happiness which God gives to a person merely by taking a soul, devoid of merit, into Heaven, there is available to His children an infinitely higher degree of happiness obtained through man's own increase in and cooperation with grace.

In other words, if a man (and there are many) were to save his soul on his deathbed after living a life of no eternal merits, that person would indeed find complete, perfect happiness on the level of eternal existence which I call the "Heaven of no Merit." However, such a person, man or woman, would be able to enjoy God's eternal glory and happiness only to the degree of capabilities of a child of say seven or eight. So, as my friend said: "Why settle for a lesser Heaven when a person can have a higher or greater Heaven?" Do not forget that Christ told us to be perfect as our heavenly Father is perfect (*Matt.* 5:48). Christ was also telling us to do all in our power to reach a higher state of union with God so as to share all the eternal rewards found in the higher degrees of happiness in Heaven.

Not only that, but only with the increase of sanctifying grace can we be better able to love and glorify God as *He deserves to be loved and glorified*. This should be our ultimate goal: to purify our souls with increase after increase of sanctifying grace so as to be better able to love, to honor, to know, to understand and to glorify God for all eternity. Only then can God give to us the most magnificent eternal treasures which He longs to give to us. Because it is His desire to bestow upon us such treasures, we owe it to Him to increase grace within our souls in order to please Him, to do His will, and to arrive at the spiritual state of union with Him which gives Him the greatest joy and pleasure.

Let me give you an example of how we must prepare our souls to receive better and richer spiritual treasures and a higher degree of union with God in Heaven simply because it is God's will that we receive such treasures and union with Him.

Say that a multimillionaire desires to share his riches and treasures with everyone who lives in his town. He tells the people to line up to receive such gifts which the man longs to give to them. He tells them that he is more than willing to fill whatever container is carried by each individual for the purpose of carrying away the treasure. He wants to fill each container to the top and he desires that each person bring the largest, tallest container the person can carry. He explains about his joy in being able to bestow upon less fortunate people treasures which they could never possess any other way.

Of course, the people bring the largest container they can carry. But what if someone stands in line with only a tiny box, or worse, no box at all! What a shame! They cannot receive all the coins and riches, which they *should* receive, simply because they are *not* prepared, they have no place to put these treasures!

With great joy, the millionaire fills each container, until he comes to the person who has only the tiny box (or no box at all). Then the generous benefactor becomes so sad, as he says: "I am so sorry, but you have such a small container (or none at all) to carry away these coins! I cannot give you all that I want to give you. You have poorly prepared yourself to receive my gifts. Now you must leave with far less than you should have had because your time for preparation has passed."

In much the same way, God cannot give you treasures if you have not prepared your soul, with His grace, to receive them. God wants you to have all these treasures in Heaven. God wants you to have the total of heavenly happiness and riches. God's greatest joy and pleasure is to give you all that He is capable of bestowing upon you. If He cannot do this, it can be said that He is sad because of your loss. If you do not prepare your soul to receive the treasures from God, which *He wants you* to have, you cannot receive them. It is grace which prepares your soul to receive God's eternal treasures; and *it is* the lack *of the increase of grace within your soul which prevents God from bestowing upon you all the treasures which are yours,* which God has reserved for you alone, which you cannot now receive.

If we do not reach the degree of perfection God wills for all of us, when Christ told us to be as perfect as His heavenly Father is (*Matt.* 5:48), then we have failed to live as God intended us to live. We have failed to gain that grace, or that increase of grace through our own fault; and this failure will mean a decrease in our happiness in Heaven.

In other words, we would not deserve Hell, for we did obtain the grace needed to save our souls, but we also would not deserve the degree of happiness in Heaven which could have been ours if only we had faithfully increased the grace within our souls, by prayer and the sacraments, and followed the command of Christ to be perfect. We would then receive a lesser degree of eternal happiness, even though it had been God's intention to reserve for us a much higher degree of eternal happiness: this degree which we will not receive because we failed to prepare our souls in a way which would entitle us to the happiness and glory God wanted to give to us.

As I said, there are different degrees or levels of happiness in Heaven. Allow me to give you another illustration of what I mean by that.

If, for example, a thousand people were sitting in the same beautiful park, seeing the very same things, such as grass, trees, flowers, the mountains and the sky, would they all be enjoying the view in the exact same way or manner? Would they all have exactly the same degree of happiness? The answer is, of course not. Each person would find happiness in this situation only to the *degree* of their personal reaction to this situation; only to the *degree* of their *personal ability* to *appreciate what it is they see.* A poet or an artist would find a joy and a happiness in the view, which could not be found by someone who would complain about the fact that he or she would rather be home watching T.V.

The amount or degree of happiness in Heaven depends upon your personal reaction to the situation called Heaven, and your personal reaction to this situation depends upon the amount of grace within your soul at the time of your death, because only with grace can your degree of ability to appreciate what you see in Heaven be increased.

Chapter 5

YOUR LOVE FOR GOD IN HEAVEN

What will be your personal reaction to the situation called Heaven? How will you see or view whatever is to be seen in Heaven? How much will you be able to appreciate, value, enjoy and understand God? How much love can you give to Him for all eternity?

Questions like these should be pondered very carefully while you are still on earth. The first thing to think about is to know that God and all treasures which are in His home can be seen, understood, appreciated and loved *only to the degree* of love which you carry with you into eternity and the amount of sanctifying grace within your soul.

As told in the little story in the last chapter, not everyone views and appreciates something like a beautiful park in the same way. Why? There are many reasons. Each person has a different intellect and abilities to understand what it is he or she sees. Each person has his or her own ideas as to what a beautiful park should look like. If the park they are in is not to their liking, they cannot enjoy it. Some people love being in a beautiful place where they can relax and rest for awhile. Other people do not know how to relax and want to go to a place where they feel "at home" with a crowd or with loud music playing.

In much the same way, souls in Heaven react differently to the situation called Heaven. The people who carry with them into eternity very little love for God combined with a small amount of sanctifying grace and no merits could never understand, love or enjoy all they see in Heaven in the same manner or to the same degree as do great saints who entered Heaven filled with pure love for God, sanctifying grace and merits. For good reason is Mary called the woman "filled with grace." It was grace which placed her upon her heavenly throne. It was love, her pure, holy love for God which she possessed that fashioned her heavenly crown of precious jewels.

You can say that God gave her gifts, blessings and graces which He does not give to us. That may be true; however, we also are given wondrous gifts from God which could bring to us numerous merits and which could increase in our souls sanctifying grace and love for God.

When you were baptized and sanctifying grace flowed into your soul for the first time, you also received three infused virtues called faith, hope and charity. Charity is also called love. With these virtues you were given the ability to know that God exists, to have faith in Him, to hope in Him, to know that you can be with Him for all eternity, and to love Him as you could never love Him without this grace and these virtues. These gifts from a loving father placed you upon the paths to a higher degree of happiness with Him forever in His Heaven of love.

However, these three virtues given at baptism were only like a tiny bud which had not as yet opened its petals to the warm sunshine. The grace was but a minute portion of what it can become by and through living a life of faith, virtue, prayer and charity.

Also, these virtues, as well as sanctifying grace, can vanish into the darkness of mortal sins. So it makes sense not only to protect the grace and virtues received at Baptism but to increase them and polish them.

As I said, a person takes into eternity only the amount of grace and merits and love for God which he or she has acquired while on earth.

It is very important to understand what that means. Christ told us to love God with our "whole heart, mind and soul" (*Matt.* 22:34:38). People may say that they do just that, but most people do not.

I have talked to or written to thousands of fallen-away Catholics and I have yet to find one who will tell me that he or she *does not love God.* All of them say they love God and want to go to Heaven. Yet, they are not willing to do what has to be done in order to prove to God how much they love Him. They do not pray, go to Mass, nor live the life of grace which a good Catholic should live. How then could such a person, with no real love for God, appreciate and understand whom it is he says he loves? And if such a person (I hope he will) saves his soul upon his deathbed, how much love can he give to God for all eternity?

Although everyone (who is in the state of grace at the moment of death) will have his whole being explode with love for God, the moment God is seen, this explosion of total love for God cannot exceed the love reserved for God alone while on earth. In other words, this love has already reached its limits. The fact that it becomes a total, a complete love for God does not mean it is a greater love for God. It means only that this love no longer is clouded or hidden behind the human limitations which just being a living human being can create. The covering has been stripped off of this love and it remains a complete love for God which, more often than not, has to be purified in Purgatory before it can be used to love God for all eternity in His Heaven of love.

When this love for God is purified in Purgatory from all traces of self-love and self-seeking, the soul will emerge from the purifying flames with his whole being filled with total love for God. However, the degree or amount of this love may be very small and so, the degree of happiness in Heaven caused by one's love for God would, of necessity, be equally as small.

For example: a diamond is a diamond, no matter what its size. The small diamond is as much of a pure diamond as a stone ten times larger. So also, all happiness in Heaven is perfect and complete—no matter what degree it is.

However, the greater the degree of happiness, the more added joys and delights a soul will be given; because, love will enable the soul to see and understand and know God—who is the source of all happiness—in a much more intimate way. The soul then will have the *ability* to fully *appreciate* what it sees, understands and knows: namely, God, His love for the soul, and the soul's love for God. This ability to appreciate is the degree of happiness which the soul will enjoy for all eternity; and this degree of happiness is based upon the amount of grace and love the soul possessed while on earth, before death. It is grace which not only increases love, increases perfection, increases merits; but, in addition, it is grace which gives the soul the ability to appreciate God and His Heaven of love to the fullest.

BIBLIOGRAPHY

A CATECHISM FOR ADULTS
Rev. William J. Cogan
Adult Catechetical Teaching Aids
4848 Clark St., Chicago, Illinois 60640

A CATHOLIC DICTIONARY
Third Edition 1961
Edited by Donald Attwater
The MacMillan Company, New York, New York

CONTEMPLATIVE LIFE IN THE WORLD
A. M. Goichon
Translated by M. A. Bouchard
B. Herder Book Co., St. Louis, Missouri

CONVERSATION WITH CHRIST
Father Peter Thomas Rohrback, O.C.D.
Fides Publishers Association
Chicago, Illinois

ENCYCLOPEDIC DICTIONARY OF THE BIBLE
Louis F. Hartman, C.SS.R.
McGraw-Hill Book Co., New York, New York

THE FAITH EXPLAINED
Leo J. Trese
Fides Publishing, Inc., Notre Dame, Indiana

HELPS AND HINDRANCES TO PERFECTION
Thomas J. Higgins, S.J.
The Bruce Publishing Co., Milwaukee, Minnesota

A HANDBOOK OF THE CATHOLIC FAITH
Van Doornik, Jelsman, Lisdonk
Image Books, A Division of Doubleday and Co., Inc.
Garden City, New York

CATHOLIC EDITION OF THE HOLY BIBLE
Confraternity—Douay Version
Catholic Book Publishing Co., New York, New York

THE JERUSALEM BIBLE
Doubleday and Co., Inc.
Garden City, New York

THE NEW AMERICAN BIBLE
Saint Joseph Edition
Catholic Book Publishing Co., New York, New York

OUR WAY TO GOD
Dr. Franz Michael William
Translated by Ronald Walls
The Bruce Publishing Co., Milwaukee, Minnesota

THE PHILOSOPHY OF ST. THOMAS AQUINAS
Etienne Gilson
B. Herder Book Co., St. Louis, Missouri

THE STATES OF PERFECTION
St. Paul Edition
By The Benedictine Monks
Daughters of St. Paul, Boston, Massachusetts

THE TEACHING OF CHRIST
Edited by Ronald Lawler, O.F.M. Cap.
Donald W. Wuerl, Thomas C. Lawler
Our Sunday Visitor, Huntington, Indiana

INTERIOR CASTLE
St. Teresa of Avila
E. Allison Peers
Image Books, A Division of Doubleday and Co., Inc.
Garden City, New York

SAINT GERTRUDE THE GREAT
HERALD OF DIVINE LOVE
Benedictine Convent of Perpetual Adoration
Clyde, Missouri

NOTES

NOTES

NOTES

NOTES